TAKEN
FOR GRANTED

TAKEN FOR GRANTED

The Future of U.S.-British Relations

Philip Seib

PRAEGER

Westport, Connecticut
London

Library of Congress Cataloging-in-Publication Data

Seib, Philip M., 1949–
    Taken for granted : the future of U.S.-British relations / Philip
Seib.
      p.   cm.
    Includes bibliographical references and index.
    ISBN 0–275–96355–1 (alk. paper)
    1. United States—Relations—Great Britain.   2. Great Britain—
Relations—United States.   3. United States—Foreign
relations—1989–   I. Title.
E183.8.G7S45   1998
303.48'273041—dc21   98–17555

British Library Cataloguing in Publication Data is available.

Library of Congress Catalog Card Number: 98–17555
ISBN: 0–275–96355–1

First published in 1998

Praeger Publishers, 88 Post Road West, Westport, CT 06881
An imprint of Greenwood Publishing Group, Inc.

Printed in the United States of America

The paper used in this book complies with the
Permanent Paper Standard issued by the National
Information Standards Organization (Z39.48–1984).

10 9 8 7 6 5 4 3 2 1

Copyright Acknowledgment

The author and publisher gratefully acknowledge permission for use of the following
material:

Excerpts from *The Downing Street Years* by Margaret Thatcher. Copyright 1993 by
Margaret Thatcher. Reprinted by permission of HarperCollins Publishers Inc. and
Margaret Thatcher.

for Christine

CONTENTS

PREFACE

When I talk to American friends about this book, the reaction is almost always the same: "Sure, the Brits need us, but do we really need them?" British friends, on the other hand, say: "The Cold War is over, and we're building a new Europe. When will America realize that it no longer is the center of the universe?"

These comments should dispel any complacency about the future of one of the world's most important friendships. For more than 200 years, the ties between Great Britain and the United States have been much like those that bind a family—sometimes loosened by spats but never altogether undone, and always fundamentally reliable. Such long-lasting relationships between nations are rare; they should be nurtured, not neglected.

During much of this century, the United States and Great Britain have joined together to wage war and preserve peace. The overall record of these efforts is one of great success: common foes have been defeated by force of arms and by resolute diplomacy. Great Britain and the United States were not the only players on the winning side, but theirs was the most stable of the Western partnerships—a sturdy foundation on which much could be built.

But alliances that were highly valued in the past may seem of little consequence in the post–Cold War era. A sense of smug invulnerability has taken hold in the West, particularly in the United States: "We won, didn't we? Now it's time to look inward."

That attitude is dangerously shortsighted. The disintegration of the Soviet Union may offer respite from fears of global nuclear war, but it certainly does not guarantee a lasting, pervasive peace. The bloody dismemberment of the former Yugoslavia is one example of the resilience of savagery. Meanwhile, new threats gestate in states with aggressive ambitions and advanced weapons.

Strategic realism is just one reason for maintaining strong ties between Great Britain and the United States. Changes in the world's economy are just as profound as the shift in the balance of military power. No nation can afford to let itself become isolated or dream of economic dominance. In the evolving global economic order, a country needs partners. The United States and Great Britain are perfect colleagues for taking advantage of this economic dynamism. Not only are their bilateral trade and investment relations strong, but also they can help each other profit from opportunities offered by the new Europe.

As desirable as cooperation between the United States and Great Britain may be, it is not essential for either country's survival today. Each could make it on its own; there is no emergency comparable to Britain's need for U.S. assistance in 1940. Nevertheless, neither country would be as successful by going it alone as it would be by acting in concert.

The case for a reinvigorated relationship between the United States and Great Britain is based on commonsense judgments about both nations' futures. It also is rooted in shared history. Although the rebellious colonial child grew up to become a superpower, language and culture remain lasting links to the British parent.

A rich past shapes the present. Today's friendship has evolved from not-so-friendly beginnings, such as British tea being dumped into Boston Harbor and British soldiers burning the U.S. president's house. Relations remained chilly through the nineteenth century and warmed only when the increasingly muscular United States joined the Allied effort in World War I.

After the Allied victory, the United States vowed that it had had enough of European wars. Twenty years later, when Great Britain came under German siege, even Winston Churchill's intense wooing of America produced only limited results. It took the attack on Pearl Harbor to propel the United States into the war and into a new military alliance with Great Britain. From that ultimately triumphant partnership emerged what Churchill and others called "the special relationship": a security arrangement that endured (with its ups and downs) throughout the Cold War. It was still firmly in place when the Soviet Union collapsed.

This past history provides ample precedent for a continued strategic partnership. Post–Cold War security needs of the United States and Great Britain lend themselves to joint action. Such action involves not only major military ventures, such as the Persian Gulf War, but also intelligence sharing, peacekeeping deployments, and "preventive maintenance" to preserve stability in Europe. Anglo-American efforts along these lines must fit into the larger scheme of security arrangements, such as those constructed by the North Atlantic Treaty Organization (NATO) and the United Nations. The expansion of NATO is certain to continue, but it is far less certain that NATO's leaders, such as the United States and Great Britain, will give appropriate attention to redefining NATO's mission, particularly with regard to sharing costs and protecting NATO members' security interests outside Europe.

Even more complicated than defense issues are economic matters. Trade between the United States and Great Britain is healthy and proceeds in a straightforward way. That, however, could change as the European Union (EU) matures. Particularly after the advent of its common currency and its likely expansion, the EU will be an economic giant requiring the United States to take a more sophisticated and respectful approach to trade relations.

Assuming that Great Britain can resolve its political problems related to its EU membership and that the United States can comprehend the scope of the EU's economic clout, the United States would benefit from having this close ally provide a convenient gateway to Europe. For its part, Great Britain can profit by offering services to U.S. companies that want to do business on the Continent, and by encouraging further U.S. investment in Great Britain. Great Britain is now the principal foreign investor in the United States (as the United States is in Great Britain) and is ideally positioned to take full advantage of a strengthened transatlantic economy.

One reason that defense and economic partnerships are feasible is the continued give-and-take between U.S. and British cultures, which have so much in common. Sometimes, however, cultural coexistence becomes a bit one-sided: Americans benefit from an infusion of Jane Austen and in exchange send *Baywatch* to Britain. Providing the "*Baywatch* babes" in return for the Bennet sisters hardly seems fair to the British.

Nevertheless, the common language has fostered a healthy shared market for music, screen, and television productions and has long made each country a favorite tourist destination for citizens of the other. This cultural common ground serves as part of the foundation on which the alliance has been built and enlarged. That has not changed appreciably so far, but as the United States becomes less "Anglo"—a demographic evolution that is proceeding rapidly—U.S.-British cultural ties may mean less to many Americans. Policy makers in both countries should consider this when they evaluate U.S. public opinion.

Other bumps exist in the road that the two countries travel. U.S. relations with Great Britain and other countries are certain to be affected by post–Cold War reappraisal of global responsibilities. "Isolationism" is too strong a word to describe the current mood, but clearly many in the United States believe that America has spent more than its share of lives and treasure during the past half-century, and now it is time for a reallocation of the burden, primarily in military matters. Similarly, trade protectionism has a considerable constituency in the United States, reinforced by politicians who play on the ignorance of many Americans about the new realities of worldwide economic competition.

Additional pressure on the U.S.-British relationship could develop if Great Britain adopts policies seen as being so Eurocentric as to be detrimental to U.S. interests. On the other side of this issue, Great Britain should resist the tug of exclusive Atlanticism; it is not a viable alternative to active participation in the EU. Just as the United States is both an Atlantic and a Pacific nation, so too should Great Britain balance its involvement with the rest of Europe and with America.

For its part, the United States needs to be sensitive about how its policies might conflict with British interests. Matters such as U.S. involvement in Northern Ireland's affairs should be handled with extreme care. Also, U.S. initiatives such as the Helms-Burton Act breed resentment among the British and others who believe that the United States is trying to bully them.

On a grander scale, the United States must decide if Great Britain is to be just another European nation or if the relationship is to remain truly special. This becomes important in U.S. dealings with other European countries, especially Germany and France. Despite the unifying influence of the EU, rivalries among its members will continue. The United States must recognize this and consider the likely ramifications if, for example, U.S. policy appears to be based on a de facto designation of Germany as the leader of Europe. Clumsiness in such matters will prove costly. The new Europe requires newly sophisticated U.S. diplomacy.

If leaders in the United States and Great Britain decide that these many issues are important and merit action, considerable work will have to be done to adjust policy and shape public opinion. Benign neglect would allow the Anglo-American relationship to grow stale, which would hamper policy makers when important coordinated decisions are to be made. Complex matters such as shaping the future of NATO could easily become mired in simplistic political controversy unless consistent, pre-emptive leadership is exercised.

Making the case for a strengthened U.S.-British relationship should not be merely a top-down process. Although presidents and prime ministers guide policy and opinion, the real base of the partnership is to be found in the steady stream of business and cultural activity that runs through the daily life of the two nations. The ties exist; they simply need to function more effectively. The task at hand involves reinforcing an existing structure, not building one from scratch.

The prognosis for U.S.-British relations remains guardedly optimistic. Alarmism is inappropriate, but so too is the assumption that a strong partnership can thrive indefinitely without thoughtful cultivation.

One stimulus for writing this book was a conversation with some U.S. officials responsible for various international economic matters. Their comments were laced with sarcastic barbs about the British, the gist of which was that "the special relationship" is nothing more than the stuff of after-dinner toasts, and that U.S. interests in Europe lie elsewhere, principally with Germany. The problem with these pronouncements was not the appraisal of German economic strength, which was accurate, but rather the dismissal of Great Britain—so absolute, so lacking in respect or regret—as if the United States can afford to push aside an ally with no concern about what that means to both countries.

My discussions with British officials were different in tone and substance. The British voiced concern about American self-centeredness and presumptuousness (Helms-Burton was often cited), but underlying their statements was an appreciation of the alliance's value. Despite the allure of the EU and the changes in NATO, there was no suggestion that close ties to the United States had lost their importance.

Neither of these viewpoints is uniform throughout the respective governments or countries, but, particularly on the U.S. side, some repair work is necessary. The Anglo-American relationship is too important to be treated cavalierly. It should not be taken for granted.

Written without benefit of a crystal ball, this book considers just some of the possible paths Anglo-American relations might follow. It is not meant to be prescriptive, but rather is designed to help frame the discussion about where this partnership is going. The first steps involve recognizing the changing dynamics of world affairs and the impact this evolution is having on the Anglo-American relationship. After doing that, those who govern and their constituencies can get down to the hard work of crafting policy.

Many people helped me think through the issues discussed in this book, and I thank them all. Among them are Dick Baly, Dick Cheney, William Crowe, Robert Culshaw, David Evans, Charles Ford, Andrew Fraser, Sandy Gardiner, Nicholas Henderson, John Holmes, Penny Holmes, Alan Hunt, Alistair Hunter, Douglas Hurd, Kay Bailey Hutchison, Kathi Kolar, David Logan, Michael Mandelbaum, Laurence Martin, Gary McDowell, Michael Mowlam, Patricia Norton, Michael O'Brien, Violet O'Hara, David Parker, Charles Powell, Philip Priestley, John Sawers, Howard Schloss, Raymond Seitz, Robert Smith, David Torrance, Graham Walker, Giles Whitaker, and Robert Worcester.

TAKEN
FOR GRANTED

CHAPTER ONE

"THE SPECIAL RELATIONSHIP"

As description, "the special relationship" is neither precise nor poetic, yet it has great staying power. When it was used most famously—by Winston Churchill in his "Iron Curtain" speech at Fulton, Missouri, in 1946—it merely amplified his call for "the fraternal association of English-speaking peoples." This meant, he said, "a special relationship between the British Commonwealth and Empire and the United States." Such a partnership, he added, would guarantee that there would be in the world "no quivering, precarious balance of power to offer its temptation to ambition or adventure." Instead, there would exist "an overwhelming assurance of security."[1]

Today, the "special relationship" between the United States and Great Britain is close and friendly, only occasionally disturbed—and then not for long—by policy disagreements. Photo-op amicability is the most familiar imagery, with president and prime minister grinning at each other at the White House or 10 Downing Street.

Often forgotten is a far less placid history, a history with its fair share of blood and passion, rivalry and distrust. The evolution of Anglo-American relations is a fascinating story in part because these two nations survived stormy times, building gradually toward current stability. Shared heritage, shared interests, and the passage of years helped heal the wounds of a revolution two centuries ago and helped the two nations forge their lasting partnership.

Although this book looks toward the future, the past should not be forgotten. What follows is a brief and highly selective history of moments that helped define this unique relationship.

DECEMBER 16, 1773

"This meeting can do nothing further to save the country." With these words from Sam Adams, a political gathering became a tea party. A band of New Englanders disguised as Indians, inspired by speeches from Adams, Josiah Quincy, and others, boarded three British merchant ships and dumped 340 chests of tea (about 90,000 pounds) into Boston Harbor.[2] The monopoly created by the Crown to benefit the East India Company would not be tolerated. The tea tax imposed by the Crown would no longer be paid.

The partygoers made their point. As the *Boston Gazette* reported, the tea dumpers had "determined to do all in their power to save their country from the ruin which their enemies had plotted. . . . The people are almost universally congratulating each other on this happy event."[3] Of this fine piece of political theater, John Adams wrote: "There is a dignity, a majesty, a sublimity, in this last effort of the patriots that I greatly admire. The people should never rise without doing something to be remembered, something notable and striking."[4]

The government in London, however, had different ideas about tea and tea parties. Although the "Mohawks" who participated in the event went unidentified, thus preventing direct retribution, British authorities had no intention of letting the incident simply pass by. The king's government contemplated a number of responses, including charging Sam Adams, John Hancock, and others with treason and having them brought to England for trial.

Eventually Parliament decided to close the port of Boston until the city indemnified the East India Company for the destroyed tea. In addition, the charter under which Massachusetts was governed was overridden to give London more control over this rambunctious colony. These measures angered even those who had thought that the Tea Partiers had gone too far. Among these was George Washington, who wrote that the new British actions were the "testimony of the most despotic system of tyranny that was ever practiced in a free government." He asked, "Shall we supinely sit and see one province after another fall a prey to despotism?"[5]

The Boston Tea Party was in part a result of a growing English arbitrariness. Benjamin Franklin, writing to a British friend in 1767, had warned that high-handedness toward the colonies would "hasten their final revolt; for the seeds of liberty are universally found there, and nothing can eradicate them."[6] His warning, and others like it, had gone unheeded.

Britain's legislative response to the Boston Tea Party changed the nature of the struggle between the colonies and England. From now on, any acts of resistance would be seen by Parliament as a direct challenge to its authority. For their part, an increasing number of Americans believed that such resistance was no longer an option but instead had become a duty.

APRIL 19, 1775

When British Marine Lieutenant Jesse Adair reached Lexington, Massachusetts, he had to decide which fork of the road to take with his column of troops. To the left was the direct route to his destination, the village of Concord. But to proceed that way would leave his flank open to the colonial militia members who were gathered, with unknown intentions, on Lexington green. If he went to the right, he would march directly at the militia. He chose the right.

A few moments later, as the troops uneasily faced each other, someone—no one knows who or on which side—fired the first shot. Then volleys were exchanged. By day's end, after the fighting in Lexington and later in Concord, the British regulars were in full retreat, harassed by the increasingly daring militia all along the road back to Boston. General Thomas Gage, commander of British forces in Massachusetts, reported 62 of his men killed, 157 wounded, and 24 missing in the day's combat.[7]

Fighting continued sporadically for most of the next year, but political change proceeded rapidly. During the first months of 1776, the Continental Congress accepted the idea of divorce from Great Britain. This became final with the Declaration of Independence, which snuffed out the hopes of the dwindling number of advocates of reconciliation on both sides of the Atlantic. The war began in earnest now, with the savage intensity of a true fight for independence rather than a short-lived uprising against authority.

Five years later, on October 19, 1781, General Charles Cornwallis surrendered his army at Yorktown, Virginia, and British hopes for victory evaporated. The vaunted British army, bulwark of the empire, had been defeated by mere rebels. The world had been turned upside down. In March 1782, the House of Commons voted to end the war, and in November negotiators agreed on the terms of a peace treaty that included British recognition of American independence.

In fairness to Lieutenant Adair, even had he chosen the left-hand fork in the road, the fighting would probably still have erupted on that April day, with the first shots fired in Concord rather than Lexington. The place did not matter; the war would begin. Britain and America were destined to live apart.

AUGUST 26, 1814

"The sky was brilliantly illumined by the different conflagrations. . . . I do not recollect to have witnessed at any period of my life a scene more striking or more sublime."[8] The scene is the city of Washington in flames. The words are those of George Robert Gleig, who as an eighteen-year-old lieutenant in the British army was part of the force that marched into Washington and burned the President's House (as the White House was then known), the Capitol, and other public buildings. Of this attack, Thomas Jefferson, in a letter to President James Madison, said, "Our enemies cannot but feel shame for their barbarous achievements at Washington."[9]

This was one of the dark incidents of the War of 1812, which was a culmination of tensions that had been growing since the Napoleonic Wars had resumed in 1803. As part of its blockade of France, the British navy seized American merchant ships and forced members of their crews to serve on British vessels. The United States responded with a series of economic measures that included a full embargo on foreign trade.

Facing mounting economic distress at home, Lord Castlereagh's government softened its treatment of the former colonies. But because of the slowness of transatlantic communication, President Madison did not learn of this change in British policy. He requested, and Congress approved, a declaration of war.

After burning Washington's public buildings, Major General Robert Ross took his troops north to Baltimore. There he encountered firm resistance; the fate of their nation's capital had stirred angry determination among Baltimore's defenders. The British fleet unsuccessfully laid siege to Fort McHenry, prompting a witness to the bombardment, Francis Scott Key, to jot down a poetic tribute to the star-spangled banner that flew defiantly above the fort.

President Madison returned to Washington the day after the British left. Rebuilding began. The war ended soon thereafter with ratification of the Treaty of Ghent, but little had been done to define the rights of U.S. vessels on the Atlantic or to decrease other tensions. The peace between the two nations remained uneasy.

FEBRUARY 13, 1842

The Boz Ball was a grand affair. Held in the Park Theater's ballroom, this was New York's tribute to its distinguished visitor, Boz himself— Charles Dickens. With food, dancing, and dramatic vignettes from Dickens's novels, the event was designed to dazzle the Englishman, and it did. In a letter to a friend at home, Dickens wrote, "The light, glitter, glare, show, noise, and cheering baffle my descriptive powers."[10]

Although Dickens was just thirty years old, he was already enormously popular on both sides of the Atlantic. On this, his first trip to the United States, he was eager to see just what kind of place the former colonies had become. For their part, his American hosts were determined to prove themselves cultured enough to meet the standards of a British literary lion. One New York newspaper, wrote Dickens, concluded its description of the Boz Ball by "gravely expressing its conviction that Dickens was never in such high society in England as he has seen in New York."[11]

Dickens accepted the acclaim with grace and good humor, but he was not so overwhelmed by the festivities that he overlooked aspects of American society that he found odious. The worst of these was slavery. In *American Notes*, which was published in England soon after he returned home, Dickens furiously attacked Americans' tolerance of slaveholding. Responding to the argument that public opinion would prevent cruel treatment of slaves, he wrote: "Public opinion, in the slave states, has delivered the slaves over to the gentle mercies of their masters. Public opinion has made the laws and denied the slaves legislative protection. Public opinion has knotted the lash, heated the branding-iron, loaded the rifle, and shielded the murderer." He also cited newspaper advertisements placed by owners of runaway slaves, such as "Ran away, a negro woman and two children. A few days before she went off, I burnt her with a hot iron on the left side of her face. I tried to make the letter M."[12]

Dickens's accounts and others like them found a receptive audience in England, where antislavery sentiment was strong. Two decades later, slavery was a major obstacle to Confederate efforts to win British support. Historian James McPherson cites reports from Confederate diplomats who found that "the public mind here is entirely opposed to the Government of the Confederate States of America on the question of slavery. . . . The sincerity and universality of this feeling embarrass the government in dealing with the question of our recognition."[13]

Despite the feelings about slavery, in May 1861, Great Britain did recognize the belligerency of the Southern states. The splintering of the United States meant, as Henry Adams wrote, "a diminution of a danger-ous power," a net strategic gain for the British.[14] The need for the South's cotton was another factor encouraging the British to meddle, as was the presence in Abraham Lincoln's cabinet of an Anglophobic secretary of state, William Seward. When a Union warship seized two Confederate emissaries from a British vessel, talk of war between the United States and Great Britain was briefly heard.

The British flirtation with the Confederate States cooled when the Emancipation Proclamation was issued. Lincoln's edict galvanized British antislavery sentiment and pushed aside other political and economic agendas. Union victories at Gettysburg and Vicksburg finished off the South's hopes for recognition.[15]

After almost a century of independence, American attitudes toward Great Britain remained mixed. Perhaps trying to shake an inferiority com-plex, the Americans could fete a Charles Dickens as a display of their cultural sophistication. They could also menace British interests to such a degree that Queen Victoria could write in her diary about the prospect of having to go to war with the United States to protect Canada.[16]

The worst conflicts were avoided, but the two nations' governments continued to eye each other warily. Meanwhile, the still-young United States continued to mature. When Charles Dickens returned to the United States in 1867 for a lengthy and triumphant visit, he offered a far kinder appraisal of his host country than he had presented twenty-five years earlier in his *American Notes*. At a New York dinner sponsored by adulatory journalists, he praised the "national generosity and magnanim-ity" that he had found while on his tour. He also told of being astounded by "the amazing changes I have seen around me on every side—changes moral, changes physical, changes in the amount of land subdued and peopled, changes in the rise of vast new cities, changes in the growth of older cities almost out of recognition, changes in the graces and amenities of life."[17] These changes in America continued at their rapid pace, and inevitably they altered the relationship between the United States and Great Britain.

JULY 20, 1895

The boundary dispute between Venezuela and British Guiana had been simmering for half a century, attracting little attention. But Great Britain's involvement in a Western Hemisphere controversy, no matter how minor, worried some avid champions of the Monroe Doctrine. They got the attention of President Grover Cleveland and his secretary of state, Richard Olney. On July 20, 1895, Olney sent a dispatch to Thomas Bayard, the U.S. ambassador to Great Britain, instructing him to press Britain to submit the dispute to arbitration. The idea itself was less offensive than the tone in which it was presented. Olney said, in part, "The Monroe Doctrine . . . rests upon facts and principles that are both intelligible and incontrovertible." He also argued that Great Britain's backing of British Guiana in the dispute "in effect deprives Venezuela of her free agency and puts her under virtual duress." Olney then asked for a British reply about arbitration by a specific date. In the nuanced language of diplomacy, this amounted to an ultimatum.[18]

The reply from Britain's prime minister, Lord Salisbury, was just as abrasive as Olney's dispatch. He defended the presence of the British flag in the Western Hemisphere and declared that the Monroe Doctrine did not have the force of international law.[19] This response infuriated Cleveland, who told Congress that the United States, not Great Britain, would define the disputed border. He also said that the U.S. government was bound to "resist by every means in its power, as a willful aggression upon its rights and interests, the appropriation by Great Britain of any lands or the exercise of any governmental jurisdiction" over Venezuelan territory. Cleveland argued that "there is no calamity which a great nation can invite which equals that which follows supine submission to wrong and injustice."[20]

This statement ignited the American jingoes. Among the more extreme was Theodore Roosevelt, then New York City police commissioner, who declared this to be a splendid opportunity for a U.S. conquest of Canada. Senator Henry Cabot Lodge raised the specter of a British plot to encircle the United States, from Caribbean outposts to infringements on the Canada-Alaska border.

In Great Britain, Cleveland's aggressiveness was viewed with dismay. The Venezuela-Guiana dispute had been seen as just another obscure diplomatic problem that would work itself out if given enough time. It was certainly not considered a crisis, at least not until the Americans proclaimed it to be one. Now, however, the stakes had been raised. Colonial Secretary Joseph Chamberlain said, "The Americans are not people to run away from."[21] The *Times* of London declared that "we must hold ourselves prepared to defend our rights in any quarter where they may be threatened."[22]

Although the Americans seemed gleefully pugnacious, military reality should have dictated greater caution. Britain's navy included forty-four battleships and forty-one cruisers; the United States had two battleships and twelve cruisers.[23] Perhaps the U.S. army could march into Canada, but control of the seas would probably be the determinative factor should the two nations actually go to war.

That prospect diminished as more sensible voices began to be heard. Among those was that of American writer Henry James, who observed, "One must hope that sanity and civilization, in both countries, will prevail."[24] Britain's Joseph Chamberlain said in a speech, "We do not covet one single inch of American territory and war between the two nations would be an absurdity as well as a crime."[25]

Eventually, Cleveland and Olney watched approvingly as Great Britain and Venezuela resolved the boundary issue. British annoyance with the United States soon faded in the face of more pressing problems. In southern Africa, Anglo-Boer relations were worsening, and German Kaiser Wilhelm decided to meddle there. That earned him a scolding from his grandmother, Queen Victoria, and led many British leaders to recognize the particular importance of transatlantic friendship if troubles with Germany were on the horizon.

The ill will engendered by the Venezuela dispute was soon set aside. As U.S. pleasure in "twisting the lion's tail" diminished, relations between Great Britain and the United States stabilized. For its part, the United States flexed its own imperial muscle, going to war against Spain and finding Great Britain quietly standing by the Americans' side. As the nineteenth century ended, the Anglo-American relationship was evolving from that of senior and junior partners to that of two equals.

DECEMBER 30, 1918

Woodrow Wilson was the first sitting American president to travel to Europe. He came as a hero, leader of the nation whose massive resources had made possible the Allies' victory in the Great War. To the huge, cheering crowds that greeted him, he was more than a triumphant warrior;

he personified a moral enlightenment that might make real the dream that this had been "the war to end all wars."

As 1918 drew to a close, Wilson spoke at the Free Trade Hall in Manchester, England, about the changing U.S. view of Europe:

> You know that the United States has always felt from the very beginning of her history that she must keep herself separate from any kind of connection with European politics, and I want to say very frankly to you that she is not now interested in European politics. But she is interested in the partnership of right between America and Europe. . . . She is not interested merely in the peace of Europe, but in the peace of the world.

He then expanded on his view of a new internationalism:

> Never before in the history of the world, I believe, has there been such a keen international consciousness as there is now. . . . There is a great compulsion of the common conscience now in existence which if any statesman resist he has gained the most unenviable eminence in history. We are not obeying the mandates of parties or of politics. We are obeying the mandates of humanity.[26]

In a speech delivered two days earlier in London, Wilson had remarked that "it has been delightful in my conferences with the leaders of your government to find how our minds moved along exactly the same line" about creating an enduring peace. He had reiterated what this meant to him: "The peoples of the world want peace and they want it now, not merely by conquest of arms but by agreement of mind."[27]

Both these speeches underscored the new role the United States had assumed. The Americans had come to Europe, belatedly in the view of some, but nevertheless committing lives and wealth to ending a conflict that had been of the Europeans' own making. Now the U.S. president was trying to shape the European peace. If Wilson had his way, British prime minister David Lloyd George and the other leaders would accept roles as supporting players and follow the U.S. lead.

The United States occupied the moral high ground, compliments of Wilson, but it also wielded new economic clout. In 1914, the United States had been a debtor nation, owing about $3.7 billion. But even before the United States entered the war, that was changing. Between

1914 and 1916, U.S. exports to Great Britain and France nearly qua-
drupled, while those to Germany dropped to almost nothing. To pay for
its massive increase in imports, Great Britain borrowed money, much of
it through the Morgan Banking House in the United States.[28] By the end
of the war, Great Britain owed almost $4 billion, while the United States
had become a creditor. Considerable financial power had moved from
London and elsewhere in Europe to New York, and the dollar had replaced the pound as the world's dominant currency.

This ascent of U.S. influence and the reshaping of the Anglo-American
relationship came to pass only after the United States had spent three
years refusing to become a combatant, a reluctance that puzzled and irritated the British. Wilson, after all, had seemed an Anglophile. As a
teenager, he had hung over his desk a portrait of British prime minister
William Gladstone. As a young scholar, he was influenced by British
political writer Walter Bagehot, whose book The English Constitution did
much to shape the style of Wilson's first book, Congressional Government.

This intellectual linkage between U.S. and British political systems did
not transcend the evolving U.S. attitudes toward Great Britain. In the
United States, pro-British sentiment was initially offset by the opposing
views of a large German-American population and by Irish Americans
who had little love for the English, especially after Britain's suppression
of the Irish rebellion in April 1916. Many Americans did not see Britain
as the mother country, and U.S. politicians were well aware of that.

U.S. entrance into the war was less a product of British persuasion than
of Germany's heavy-handed ineptitude. If the Germans had renounced
unrestricted submarine warfare and if they had even pretended to be more
amenable to negotiations, Wilson might have left Europe to the Europeans. They did not, so he did not.

With the war won, British and other European leaders promptly began
devising ways to end their dependence on U.S. largesse and to neutralize
Wilson, who was seen by many European politicians as sanctimonious
and unrealistic. Evidence of the private attitude toward the American
president can be found in the secret minutes of the Imperial War Cabinet,
which met in London on the same day Wilson was delivering his stirring
speech in Manchester. The meeting reviewed Wilson's visit to Britain
and the discussions he had had with Lloyd George and others.

The prime minister reported that the president "had given the impression that [the League of Nations] was the only thing that he really
cared much about." Lloyd George also dismissed Wilson's commitment

to the third of the Fourteen Points, which called for free trade, saying that "President Wilson meant nothing in particular by that article anyhow, and since he had brought it forward he had lost the [congressional] election in the United States."[29]

Other members of the War Cabinet were even more caustic. Lord Curzon, soon to become foreign secretary, said that unless Wilson became more specific than he had been during his talks with British officials, "the Peace Conferences would be a dreary fiasco."[30] Australian prime minister William Morris Hughes said "that if we were not very careful we would find ourselves dragged quite unnecessarily behind the wheels of President Wilson's chariot." Hughes, while professing gratitude for the Americans' war role, argued that the United States "had made no money sacrifice at all" and "had not even exhausted the profits they had made" before entering the war. Hughes further said that "it was intolerable for President Wilson to tell us that the world was to be saved on his terms. If the saving of civilization had depended on the United States, it would have been in tears and chains today."[31] More moderate voices were also heard in the War Cabinet, but Lloyd George and others clearly were wary of strong American leadership in making the peace and in shaping postwar geopolitics.

Regardless of the British officials' private condescension toward Wilson, the military and economic power of the United States had become incontrovertible fact. The United States was ready to assert itself as the leader in the relationship with Great Britain.

SEPTEMBER 10, 1940

"This is London. And the raid which started about seven hours ago is still in progress."[32] On this third night of the London blitz, the message was about friends under siege. The messenger was Edward R. Murrow, using radio to give Americans their first "living-room war." Murrow sent across the Atlantic the sounds of air-raid sirens and antiaircraft fire and German bombs, the click of Londoners' footsteps on the battered sidewalks, and the eerie silence that hung in the air until the next wave of bombers arrived. He told the story of the British—not the generals and politicians, but the shopkeepers and housewives and others who huddled at night in crowded shelters as their city was pounded and then the next morning continued their lives. In a broadcast the following spring, Murrow said:

There is great courage and a blind belief that Britain will survive.
. . . During a blinding raid when the streets are full of smoke and
the sound of the roaring guns, they'll say to you, "Do you think
we're really brave, or just lacking in imagination?" Well, they've
come through the winter; they've been warned that the testing days
are ahead. Of the past months, they may well say, "We've lived a
life, not an apology." And of the future, I think most of them would
say, "We shall live hard, but we shall live."[33]

That mix of reporting and romanticism, combined with the vast reach
of radio, caught the attention of the American audience. The European
war became less an esoteric political exercise and more a human drama.
Murrow's broadcasts apparently had effect. A Gallup poll in September
1940 found that only 16 percent of Americans favored providing more
aid to Great Britain. A month later, with the devastating effects of the
blitz better known, that number had risen to 52 percent.

Reports about the blitz helped Franklin Roosevelt as he cautiously tried
to reshape American public opinion. Isolationism was a shrill and potent
political force, with its champions such as aviator Charles Lindbergh is-
suing stern warnings about repeating "the error of 1917" by marching to
Europe's rescue. In 1935, the Neutrality Act had been passed over-
whelmingly by Congress, prohibiting any U.S. military aid to belligerents
in any war between foreign states. The following year, the measure was
expanded to prohibit bankers from lending money to warring nations.
Roosevelt said that such constraints on U.S. action "played right into the
hands of the aggressor nations," but it was not until the Russo-German
Non-Aggression Pact of 1939 that the United States began to show signs
of recognizing reality.

Also in 1939, King George VI became the first reigning British sov-
ereign to visit the United States. The king and Queen Elizabeth were
warmly received. Roosevelt turned on the charm and plied the royal cou-
ple with hot dogs when they visited his Hyde Park home. Despite the
showmanship of the royal visit, the most pressing business for Roosevelt
was winning reelection in 1940. Winston Churchill understood this, saying, "I fear that isolationism is the winning ticket."[34]

There was, however, a change coming. Roosevelt's shrewd, if cautious,
maneuvering and Murrow's quietly impassioned portraits of British her-
oism were among the factors leading Americans toward helping their
friends. A year before the United States entered the war, Murrow provided his listeners with this analysis:

It's possible that for a time certain Britishers believed that American aid on a neutral basis would be adequate and effective. If they thought so, their disillusionment has been rapid. Ask any member of Parliament or any member of the government whether he prefers a neutral America or a belligerent America, and you will get only one answer. Some would express a preference for winning the war without American aid, but most would admit that it can't be done.[35]

As had been the case a quarter-century before, Great Britain needed help, and it could only come from across the Atlantic.

AUGUST 12, 1941

The British warships were the first to depart, steaming away from Placentia Bay and the Newfoundland coast. They were heading for Iceland and then on to Great Britain, wary of the U-boats that might be lying in wait in the North Atlantic. Soon thereafter, the U.S. ships also got under way for their shorter trip home. Aboard the battleship *Prince of Wales* was Winston Churchill. Franklin Roosevelt was on the cruiser *Augusta*. The two men had just concluded a conference setting forth, in a carefully unofficial way, the aims of a war in which the United States was increasingly involved, also in a carefully unofficial way.

In this first meeting between the prime minister and the president, the two men got along well. On the question of U.S. aid for the British war effort, Churchill gently tugged and Roosevelt politely resisted, giving some ground but not as much as Churchill wanted. Nevertheless, their discussions produced the Atlantic Charter, a document both idealistic and pragmatic. It stated principles on which the two nations based "their hopes for a better future for the world," and began by pledging that both countries would "seek no aggrandizement, territorial or other." It further called for self-determination, open seas, and "after the final destruction of the Nazi tyranny . . . the abandonment of the use of force."[36] The document was brief but sophisticated, calling for a peace with enforcement mechanisms and for treaty terms with Germany that would not be provocatively crippling. The two leaders understood the folly of the Versailles Treaty of 1919 and were, even at this early point, determined to do better.

After returning home, Churchill told Great Britain about the meeting in a radio broadcast. He acknowledged that the United States was "the most powerful state and community in the world" and described the re-

lationship between "the British Empire and the United States, who, for-
tunately for the progress of mankind, happen to speak the same language
and very largely think the same thoughts." The shipboard conference, he
said, symbolized "in a form and manner which everyone can understand
. . . the deep underlying unities which stir and, at decisive moments, rule
the English-speaking peoples throughout the world."[37]

This, then, in Churchill's view, was the foundation of the alliance: the
shared culture and the values that took root in that common ground. The
English-speaking peoples, said Churchill, "without any clog of selfish interest," would lead "the toiling masses in all the continents . . . forward
out of the miseries into which they have been plunged, back to the broad
high-road of freedom and justice."[38]

The Atlantic Charter took the U.S.-British relationship a step forward.
As Churchill later wrote, "The fact alone of the United States, still technically neutral, joining with a belligerent power in making such a declaration was astonishing."[39] But Churchill still had to deal with U.S.
reluctance to enter the war officially. He reported to his war cabinet that
Roosevelt would "wage war if not declare it," but Roosevelt told the U.S.
public that the conference had brought the United States "no closer to
war."

Churchill was extremely uneasy about Britain moving into 1942 alone,
but Roosevelt was playing a cautious political game, nudging the U.S.
public toward greater belligerency. At some political risk, he had in 1940
pushed through the Lend-Lease program to get Britain some desperately
needed military hardware. Churchill later called this "the most unselfish
and unsordid financial act of any country in all history."[40] Roosevelt
would not do much more than that, and certainly not as much as Churchill wanted. An opinion poll taken soon after the Atlantic meeting
found that 74 percent of Americans remained opposed to entering the
war.[41]

A month after the Atlantic Conference, however, an exchange of fire
between a German submarine and an American destroyer let Roosevelt
take another step ahead. Declaring the need to take assertive action "in
the waters which we deem necessary for our defense," Roosevelt ordered
U.S. vessels to "shoot on sight" at any German or Italian warships. The
president told a national radio audience: "We have sought no shooting
war with Hitler. We do not seek it now. . . . But when you see a rattle-
snake poised to strike, you do not wait until he has struck before you
crush him."[42]

Roosevelt's prowar efforts were being aided not solely by Americans' support for Britain, but also by growing antipathy toward Hitler. Earlier in 1941, Churchill had told the United States, "Give us the tools, and we will finish the job," but Roosevelt, according to historian Robert Dallek, believed that direct U.S. naval and air involvement would be necessary to stop the Germans.[43]

U.S. public opinion changed once and for all when the Japanese attacked Pearl Harbor on December 7, 1941. But even when the United States entered the war, helping Britain was not the concern of most Americans. A poll taken two months after Pearl Harbor found that 62 percent of the public favored concentrating all or most of the war effort against the Japanese, while only 25 percent wanted to make Germany the principal target.[44] Churchill had come to the United States immediately after the U.S. declaration of war. Addressing a joint session of Congress, Churchill praised the United States for having "drawn the sword for freedom and cast away the scabbard."[45]

Roosevelt and Churchill were perhaps the two greatest political leaders of the twentieth century, and their partnership was a close one. After Roosevelt's death in 1945, Churchill noted that they had exchanged more than 1,700 messages and had met nine times for a total of about 120 days. In the eulogy he delivered in the House of Commons, Churchill said that Roosevelt had been "the greatest American friend we have ever known, and the greatest champion of freedom who has ever brought help and comfort from the new world to the old."[46]

During the war, the New World had again proved able to determine the fortunes of the Old. In the peace of sorts that followed, the New World's dominance continued. The retreat from responsibility that had taken place after the previous world war would not occur again. Ties between Great Britain and the United States were closer than ever before, and now the United States found itself with more authority than it had ever possessed—or wanted—in the past.

NOVEMBER 4, 1956

The telegram from the British prime minister to the American president was deferentially plaintive: "The future of all of us depends on the closest Anglo-American cooperation. It has, of course, been grave to me to have had to make a temporary breach into it which I cannot disguise, but I know that you are a man of big enough heart and vision to take up things again on the basis of fact."[47] That was Anthony Eden's attempt to assuage Dwight Eisenhower as Great Britain's seizure of the Suez Canal was falling apart in the face of U.S. opposition. The plan had seemed so clever: induce Israel to attack Egypt, and then send in a British-French "peacekeeping" force to separate the Israelis and Egyptians and take control of the canal. The ploy, however, was so transparent that it deceived no one, least of all the Americans, who were furious both about the plan's flaws and about not having been consulted. Making matters worse, this act of old-fashioned imperial aggression provided splendid political cover for the Soviet Union, which was in the process of brutally crushing an uprising in Hungary.

In addition to being the "temporary breach" in the Anglo-American partnership that Eden described, the British action illustrated a fundamental divergence in the two nations' foreign policies. Great Britain seemed to be having a delusion of grandeur past, assuming that it could send troops into Egypt as if they were chasing Napoleon, and caring little about what the rest of the world thought. The British also assumed that the Americans, despite their unhappiness about not being informed, would ultimately stand by their ally.

The United States, however, was determined to be more circumspect in dealings with Egyptian nationalist leader Gamal Abdel Nasser, even if the Eisenhower administration had not fully determined the specifics of its policy. The Dulles brothers, Secretary of State John Foster and Central Intelligence Agency Director Allen, were pursuing their own very distinct Nasser strategies. Allen Dulles believed that the Egyptian leader was pliable and worth dealing with. His brother thought that Nasser was doing Moscow's work and should be removed, if that could be done without leaving fingerprints. Within the administration, the secretary of state's view eventually prevailed.[48]

Although U.S. policy toward Egypt was neither friendly nor coherent, it was moving along a far different track than was Great Britain's. In the contest with the Soviet Union for influence among nonaligned nations in Africa and elsewhere, Eisenhower recognized the dangers of overt strong-arm ventures such as the Suez incursion. The theory, if not always the practice, of U.S. foreign policy was becoming more sophisticated.

Great Britain had good reason to worry about control of the canal. Without the shortcut it provided, thousands of miles would be added to the journey of the Middle Eastern oil on which Britain depended, making it prohibitively expensive. Therefore, when Nasser nationalized the canal, the Eden government reacted frantically.

Eisenhower's angry disapproval of the Anglo-French scheme was not something Eden could simply shrug off. The crisis weakened the British pound in international financial markets, and the United States made matters worse by refusing to protect it, selling some of its own sterling reserves, and not approving Britain's request to withdraw funds from the International Monetary Fund (IMF).[49] After initially blocking Eden, the United States offered Britain an emergency loan, but only if a cease-fire and withdrawal were ordered immediately. Eden had no choice; he had to accept. Less than twenty-four hours after the Anglo-French force had landed in Egypt, the prime minister called the French and admitted that their enterprise was a failure. Soon thereafter, the United States became helpful. Britain received oil, a $500-million credit from the Export-Import Bank, and IMF assistance. Britain's economy steadied.[50]

In the U.S.-British relationship, there could be no doubt where the most power rested: in Washington, not London. The British government was learning that it would have to defer to U.S. interests when contemplating endeavors such as the Suez seizure. Although fifteen years earlier Churchill had needed to cajole Roosevelt into helping a desperate Britain, that relationship was basically one between equals, with each side usually observing the appropriate political niceties. Now Eisenhower was making clear that the British were out of line and should not expect automatic U.S. backing for their foreign policy adventures. U.S. diplomat Robert Murphy had reported that as the crisis developed, it was clear that Eden "had not adjusted his thoughts to the altered world status of Great Britain, and he never did."[51]

Despite the discord, this episode also underscored how important the partnership remained. Both sides were at fault for letting the collegial relationship fall into disrepair, but they remained linked by the common goal of foiling the Soviet Union. As George Kennan later observed, "The state of Anglo-American relations at the time of Suez, aside from being veritably tragic in the paralysis it inflicted on Western policy toward the Hungarian rebellion, represented a low point in the entire development of American policy in the postwar period."[52]

Although Eisenhower was exasperated by what he called the "mess and botch of things" in the Suez crisis, he did not let the Anglo-American partnership drift into further difficulties. He wrote to Winston Churchill, "I shall never be happy until our old-time closeness has been restored."[53] When Harold Macmillan succeeded Eden, relations began to improve. Macmillan's mother was American, and he and Eisenhower had become friends during World War II. In March 1957, the two leaders met in Bermuda and, because they liked and trusted each other, promptly repaired the relationship between their countries. As tangible evidence of this improvement, the United States later that year granted Britain the right to receive technical information and fissile material for producing nuclear warheads. No other nation received this assistance.

With relations warmer, an effective Cold War partnership was again in place, but it was not a partnership of equals. Henry Kissinger has observed that "it was under Macmillan that Great Britain completed the transition from power to influence."[54] Implicitly, both nations recognized that on matters of mutual concern the United States would lead and Great Britain would follow.

NOVEMBER 16, 1988

It was clear on this nostalgic occasion that the affection the president and the prime minister professed for one another was very real, reaching beyond their shared conservative politics. They had stood together for eight years while the world had changed. Now, as Ronald Reagan prepared to leave the White House, he wanted his last official visitor to be the same person who had been his first: Margaret Thatcher.

Thatcher had first come in February 1981, a month after Reagan became president. During that visit, she spoke about an Anglo-American partnership that would "promote stability, prevent aggression, and oppose tyranny." She said then at the White House, "The message I have brought across the Atlantic is that we in Britain stand with you. . . . Your problems will be our problems, and when you look for friends we will be there."[55] That promise was to be tested, but it always, in the end, was kept.

Just a year after that first friendly meeting, the relationship endured its most severe strain since the Suez crisis of 1956. After a century-long ownership dispute, Argentina seized the Falkland Islands, 8,000 miles from England but home to 2,000 British subjects (and their many sheep). Thatcher dispatched British warships and troops to reclaim the territory.

This created a dilemma for the Reagan administration. Although there may have been an inclination to stand by the longtime ally, the realities of Western Hemisphere politics made this difficult. The United States was trying to shed its image of "gringo imperialism," and to side with a European power against a Latin American state would be a massive setback for that effort. Secretary of State Alexander Haig tried to mediate the dispute, but to no avail. Even after British troops had landed on the islands, Reagan attempted to convince Thatcher to stop the offensive and let diplomats take over. She would have none of it and told the president so bluntly.[56]

Reagan faced a division within his own ranks. For example, the views of pro-British Secretary of Defense Caspar Weinberger were countered by those of United Nations Ambassador Jeane Kirkpatrick, who believed that the British had overreacted and who argued that Reagan should be more concerned about Latin American sentiments. With Reagan's foreign policy team split about what course to take, the administration looked increasingly like a befuddled bystander as events proceeded. Beneath the political surface, however, the United States was supporting the British military effort. Haig and White House national security adviser William Clark privately told Nicholas Henderson, Great Britain's ambassador to Washington, that they and the president were firmly on Britain's side.[57]

Beyond these assurances, the most important contribution was a supply of Sidewinder air-to-air missiles, which gave the British clear superiority in the air. As British journalist John Dickie has reported, the United States also supplied the British with six million gallons of aviation fuel, shoulder-held Stinger missiles, Shrike antiradar missiles, Harpoon antiship missiles, mortar and artillery ammunition, air-drop containers, helicopter engine parts, and more. All this was done quietly and was expedited because of the support of Secretary Weinberger. Also, Central Intelligence Agency Director William Casey made his agency's gleanings available to his British counterparts.[58]

Despite protestations of impartiality, U.S. policy during the Falklands War had this decided pro-British tilt because the Anglo-American relationship was judged to be a valuable long-term investment, more important than a speculative effort to curry favor in Latin America. From Britain's standpoint, U.S. support proved essential in achieving the favorable military outcome.[59]

In October 1983, Reagan and Thatcher were again in disagreement about military action, this time a venture far smaller in scale than the Falklands War had been. At the request of the Organization of Eastern Caribbean States, the United States sent troops into Grenada to dislodge a pro-Cuban leader and protect about 1,000 American citizens who were on the island, many of whom were attending a medical school there. Grenada is a member of the British Commonwealth, and although Britain had indicated that it would not involve itself in the country's political turmoil, the Thatcher government expected to be consulted before the United States took unilateral action. Communication between Washington and London about this matter was remarkably inefficient, leaving Foreign Secretary Geoffrey Howe in the embarrassing position of telling the House of Commons that he knew of no American intervention plans even as the military operation was about to get under way.[60]

Thatcher wrote in her memoirs that she felt "dismayed and let down by what had happened. At best, the British Government had been made to look impotent; at worst we looked deceitful." She had to explain to Parliament "how it had happened that a member of the Commonwealth had been invaded by our closest ally."[61]

In Washington, Reagan was chagrined by Thatcher's opposition. As Secretary of State George Shultz recorded in his memoirs, Reagan "had supported her in the Falklands. He felt he was absolutely right about Grenada. She didn't share his judgment at all. He was deeply disappointed."[62]

By going into Grenada, Reagan was telling not just Cuba but also the Soviet Union, Syria, and other nations that the United States was not averse to using military force when it felt that even its peripheral security interests were threatened. Thatcher, although she had harshly criticized the U.S. action when speaking in the House of Commons, later acknowledged that the intervention had been a success.[63]

The realities of Anglo-American consultation were underscored by this small crisis. Reagan saw the Grenada decision as a matter of U.S. policy, certainly not requiring approval from London. Granted that the British should not have been misled, as they apparently were initially, he viewed notification of Thatcher as a courtesy, nothing more. He was taken aback by Thatcher's presumption that she would play a substantive role in determining whether the United States would take military action.

In 1986, the relationship was tested in yet another military situation. Again, the United States was about to launch a military operation, but this time it officially requested British help. The target was Libya: an air attack in response to a series of terrorist bombings, including one in Berlin that U.S. intelligence agencies had convincingly argued had been orchestrated by Muammar Qaddafi's government. Reagan wanted Thatcher's permission to launch the raid, to be carried out by U.S. F-111 jets, from NATO bases in England.

Initially, Thatcher and her advisers were hesitant. They responded not with a "yes" or "no," but with a list of questions. After the Americans provided thorough answers, Thatcher gave her approval, even though she knew that by doing so she would likely suffer politically at home and open Britain to reprisals in the Middle East. According to her aide Charles Powell, Thatcher's cabinet balked, but she said: "This is what allies are for. If you're an ally, you're an ally. If one wants help, they get help."[64]

The U.S. attack proved less precise than promised. Some bombs missed their targets. Civilians were killed or wounded. Americans nevertheless supported Reagan's move; the polls showed 77 percent approving. But in Great Britain, roughly 70 percent of those polled said that Thatcher should not have cooperated.[65] The prime minister, however, did not second-guess herself. She agreed with Reagan's view that countries sponsoring terrorism must be shown that they could not do so without paying a price. In her memoirs, she wrote: "Whatever the cost to me, I knew that the cost to Britain of not backing American action was unthinkable. If the United States was abandoned by its closest ally the American people and their government would feel bitterly betrayed—and reasonably so."[66]

Thatcher's standing with the American president and the American public rose after this incident. Particularly when contrasted with France, which had refused to let the American planes fly over French air space, Great Britain appeared to be the one ally on whom the United States could count.

Beyond this series of military tests, the Reagan-Thatcher relationship was most important in the unified front it presented to the Soviet Union. While the other European allies of the United States became nervous when Reagan challenged the Soviets, Thatcher tended to remain supportive. She was generally in philosophical agreement with Reagan's definition of the Soviet Union as "an evil empire" and with the "Reagan doctrine" that prescribed aggressive countermeasures against Communist troublemaking. That was why she was standing with Reagan on the White House lawn in November 1988.

In some respects, this had been the Cold War version of the Roosevelt-Churchill partnership. In both cases, the relationship had been strengthened because Great Britain and the United States faced a common adversary—in the first instance the Axis powers, and in the second the Soviet Union. In both cases, the Anglo-American alliance prevailed.

It may turn out that this kind of personalized partnership is obsolete. Thatcher noted in her memoirs that Reagan's successor, George Bush, wasted little time in distancing himself from her. In her book, she recited a litany of praise for Bush, but added that "he had never had to think through his beliefs and fight for them when they were hopelessly unfashionable as Ronald Reagan and I had had to do." Aside from a personal coolness in relations with Bush, she detected a new U.S. favoritism toward Germany at the expense of Great Britain.[67]

Bush remained polite in all his dealings with Thatcher, but not until

Iraq invaded Kuwait in August 1990 did their relationship achieve its greatest importance. Thatcher bolstered Bush's resolve to take firm action against Saddam Hussein, at one point telling the president, "This is no time to go wobbly."

That was one of Thatcher's final contributions. She had expected to direct British participation in a Persian Gulf war. Like Churchill, she anticipated doing so in close partnership with the American president. But politics intervened. Also like Churchill, after a lengthy tenure she found herself unable to prevail in political battles at home. On November 22, 1990, almost exactly two years after saying farewell to Ronald Reagan at the White House, Thatcher announced that she was resigning as prime minister.

MAY 29, 1997

They stood together in the sun-dappled garden of 10 Downing Street, the young American president and the even younger British prime minister. Of the duo, Bill Clinton at fifty was the elder statesman, a fact reinforced by his graying hair and the cane he used as he recovered from knee surgery. Tony Blair, forty-four, bright and eager as always, clearly relished the parity of the joint news conference.

Before becoming prime minister, Blair had recognized the changing dynamic in Anglo-American ties. "The Americans have made it clear," he said, "that they want a special relationship with Europe, not with Britain alone."[68] He also said:

I do not believe we have to choose between Europe and America. No other European country would dream of doing so. In fact, the two relationships are crucially interdependent.

We need to understand that the nature of our relationship with the U.S. has changed. It was always bound to do so after the end of the Cold War. Politico-military issues were at the core, but today economic issues have taken on greater weight. The Europeans no longer have the same incentive to exercise leadership on every issue—nor do they always see as clearly the direction in which they should lead. . . .

Britain has to understand that its strength comes from its position at the junction of these two relationships. They should not be looked at separately. The key is the way they interlock and reinforce each other. Europe is not an alternative to the transatlantic relationship. . . . Our influence in each is crucial to our influence in the other. It is only if we are at the heart of decision-making in Europe that we will be taken seriously in Washington. And it is only if we have a new, strong, post–Cold War relationship with the U.S. that we will have the same degree of influence in Europe.

Blair also recognized the change in America's worldview: "I do not believe that the U.S. will turn in on itself in a return to the isolationism of the 1930s, and I strongly welcome President Clinton's assurance on this point. But it will be more difficult to get the U.S. interested in overseas activities. Americans will have to be convinced that their interests are engaged."[69]

Clinton had previously shown himself sensitive to the historic durability of U.S. ties to Britain. In a November 1995 speech to the British Parliament, Clinton said: "Other times in other places are littered with the vows of friendship sworn during battle and then abandoned in peacetime. This one stands alone, unbroken, above all the rest; a model for the ties that should bind all democracies."[70]

Now, together in London, the two men put their generational and political unity on display. Just a few weeks earlier, Blair's Labour party had won a landslide election victory. He took office with a majority of 179 in the House of Commons, which meant that whatever legislative program he wanted, he could have. Clinton could only ponder that enviously. He was the leader of the most powerful nation on earth, but his power within his own government was no match for that which Blair wielded.

In his opening remarks at the news conference, Blair reported on his discussions with Clinton, reiterating themes he had espoused before his election. The two agreed, he said, "that Britain does not need to choose between being strong in Europe or being close to the United States of America, but that by being strong in Europe we will further strengthen our relations with the U.S." Blair said that he and Clinton also agreed "that this is a new era which calls for a new generation politics and a new generation leadership. This is the generation that prefers reason to doctrine, that is strong in ideals but is indifferent to ideology, whose instinct is to judge governments not on grand designs but on practical results."[71] Blair's citing an indifference to ideology illustrated how much had changed since the Reagan-Thatcher days. For his part, Clinton respectfully acknowledged the "unique partnership" between the United States and Great Britain and the "unbreakable alliance . . . based on shared values and common aspirations."[72] He and Blair presented what seemed to be a comfortably united front on NATO expansion and other issues.

The camaraderie of this occasion underscored the similarities in the two men's backgrounds and political outlooks. Each attended Oxford, each is a lawyer married to a lawyer, and each pulled his political party away from a self-defeating liberalism and onto the middle ground where elections can be won. Each is a shrewd, skillful politician who understands the importance of consensus building in domestic politics and presumably recognizes the need for the same in the international arena. At the outset, every indication was that this would be a politically and personally close, congenial partnership.

The Anglo-American relationship has come a long way since the Boston Tea Party. The rebellious colonies have matured to become a superpower, but ties to the mother country, although greatly changed, have never been broken. The ups and downs of two centuries of shared history produced a firm and powerful friendship.

Although only a few years separated the Reagan-Thatcher and Clinton-Blair relationships, the enormous changes in the world during that time have made the nature of cooperation intrinsically different. Throughout most of the twentieth century, Anglo-American ties had drawn strength from necessity—the need to face, and sometimes to fight, common foes. With victories in two world wars and the Cold War, the United States and Great Britain had proved themselves to be a formidable team. The mutual benefits accruing to this partnership more than outweighed the occasional problems.

British diplomat and historian Harold Nicolson wrote of Europe after the Congress of Vienna, "History teaches us, and invariably we disregard her lesson, that coalitions begin to disintegrate from the moment the common danger is removed."[73] With the principal common danger, a menacing Soviet Union, having been removed, the test now for the United States and Great Britain is to take to heart history's lesson that has so often been disregarded and preserve a special relationship.

CHAPTER TWO

DEFENDERS OF THE FAITH

For most of the twentieth century, shared security interests have been among the most dominant factors in the Anglo-American partnership. When Winston Churchill talked about "the special relationship" in his 1946 "Iron Curtain" speech, he emphasized the importance of close ties between the armed forces of the two countries, the joint use of military bases, and other measures to ensure that Great Britain and the United States would present a united front to any adversary. This linkage was the cornerstone of NATO and did much to shape the West's overall Cold War defense strategy. Although debate continues about what aspects of that strategy proved the most successful, the outcome is beyond dispute: the West won the Cold War.

That was a marvelous accomplishment, but the dissolution of the Soviet Union removed the principal raison d'être of NATO and various subsidiary military relationships, including that between the United States and Great Britain. After almost half a century of common purpose, suddenly there is a need to redefine goals.

Some players want new roles. The French, for example, want more respect. They have tried to be more assertive in European defense planning and have made the case that the outcome of a defense-industrial competition between Europe and the United States will determine the extent of Europe's independence. Europe, the French contend, should become more self-sufficient in producing its own defense hardware. Also, to reduce reliance on the United States, Europe's military powers should improve their own satellite intelligence, airlift capabilities, and other tactical tools.

France indicated in 1997 that it wanted to supersede the U.S. role in some areas. For instance, French president Jacques Chirac pledged to integrate France's military into NATO, but wanted the United States in return to accept an independent European command in the Mediterranean. The Clinton administration, however, was firmly unreceptive. The U.S. attitude is that France would benefit from rejoining NATO and would remain at a disadvantage by continuing to be an outsider. Therefore, the French are not in a position to dictate terms.

As the participants have changed, so too has the language of geopolitics been altered. "Superpower," if defined in military terms, has little meaning when there is only one. "Alliance" is a less muscular word if there is no one to ally against. Whether figurative or literal, the metamorphosis taking place since the end of the Cold War is part of the politics of victory.

Another task at hand is to find an answer to the question "Now what?" The philosophy that held the West together had two principal facets: communism is bad, and democracy is good. With the former moot, what does the latter mean? It is still accepted as true, but it needs much more heft if it is to be the basis for a resilient post–Cold War philosophy. "Democratic reforms" are expected from Eastern European countries that want to join NATO and the European Union, but the standards for such reforms remain imprecise.

Likely to evolve is a modus vivendi that is more pragmatic than ideological, placing more emphasis on political stability and economic growth and less on military clout and underlying philosophy. But without the need to provide counterpoint to an opposing doctrine, proponents of this approach may find that its advancement suffers from lack of perceived urgency. In practical terms, this means that policy makers may be hard pressed to convince their governments or the public that a particular action is necessary.

THE SEARCH FOR STABILITY

Stability is an alluring goal, but it can smother constructive dynamism and produce a false sense of security. Margaret Thatcher has observed that "stability should not be used as an excuse for upholding a status quo that is itself inherently unstable because it suppresses social forces that cannot ultimately be contained."[1]

During the Cold War, anticommunism was a convenient, all-purpose rationale. Want to deploy Pershing missiles in Europe? Make the case that they are an essential check on Soviet expansionism. Want to send troops into Grenada? Point out that the island's government has been taken over by Marxists. Want to send arms to Afghan rebels? Justify it as a way to irritate the Kremlin. Many of the West's foreign policy initiatives for fifty years were based—in argument if not always in fact—on the premise that they were essential to counter the menace of "the other side."

Whether referred to as containment or something else, this strategy also brought a certain logic to the geography of the Cold War. Much of Europe was cleanly divided into the domains of NATO and the Warsaw Pact. Gradually, the Kremlin's influence over some of its satellites began to crumble, particularly as it became clear that the Soviet leadership had neither the resolve nor the ability to act as aggressively as it had in Hungary in 1956 and Czechoslovakia in 1968. In those two countries, as well as in Poland, East Germany, and elsewhere in Eastern Europe, the 1980s saw the Soviet Union's grip loosen, then slip, and eventually release.

Despite this remarkable change, the notion that there would now be a Pax Europa was quickly dispelled. The disintegration of what had been Yugoslavia and the bloody tumult in some of the former Soviet states proved that the end of the Cold War did not mean the end of war in Europe. These new conflicts raised the question of who, if anyone, has policing responsibilities. NATO and the Western European Union were established military alliances, but they had been designed to defend Europe against a Soviet attack, not to lean on disruptive neighbors. The United States, in particular, was faced with the task of redefining its NATO and overall European role.

For Great Britain and the other Western European powers, the task was only slightly less complicated. Unlike the United States, which could conceivably wash its hands of Europe and depart, they did not have the option of simply walking away; they had nowhere to walk to. New spheres of influence would have to be defined, at least implicitly. Historic ties in themselves would not be a sufficient basis for this; in fact, relying on such grounds for new relationships could exacerbate problems, as happened in the Balkans, with Germany embracing Croatia and Russia feeling protective toward the Serbs. Only by consistently acting in concert might

European states avoid at least some of the problems caused by assertion of self-interest. Such unity, however, has been achieved only sporadically.

U.S. ATTITUDES

Consistent unity and consistent U.S. participation may be unlikely, but they are especially necessary in developing a policy toward Russia. This may prove to be the most crucial component in constructing a peaceful future for Europe, and it may be the most important venue for jointly exercised leadership from Washington and London.

But even with regard to Russia, and certainly with regard to the rest of Europe, the United States may turn out to be laggard more than leader mainly because of domestic public opinion. Although "isolationist" is too strong a term to describe Americans' attitude toward the rest of the world, "inward-looking" is not. So far, there is not significant popular support for disengagement, but neither is there anything more than a fragile commitment behind an active U.S. presence in European affairs.

A 1994 survey commissioned by the Chicago Council on Foreign Relations found that 56 percent of the public wanted to maintain the current level of U.S. commitment to NATO, while only 26 percent wanted to decrease it. But an endorsement is one thing; willingness to back it up is something else. Among those polled, only 54 percent of the public favored using U.S. troops if Russia invaded Western Europe, and only 32 percent if Russia invaded Poland.[2]

Polling conducted in January 1997 for the Pew Research Center for the People and the Press found 61 percent of the public in favor of maintaining NATO—roughly the same level of support since 1991. By a margin of 45 percent to 40 percent, respondents endorsed NATO expansion. This same survey found the public ranking domestic policy more important than foreign policy, 86 percent to 7 percent.[3]

Another survey conducted for the Pew Center in September 1997 found that "most Americans fundamentally doubt the relevance of international events to their own lives." A significant minority of the survey's respondents, 39 percent, agreed with the assertion "The U.S. should mind its own business internationally and let other countries get along the best they can on their own," while 54 percent disagreed.[4]

This softness of public resolve was reflected in the Clinton administration's careful footwork as it developed its policy about intervention in the former Yugoslavia. Regardless of judgments about the quality of Clinton's foreign policy generally, on this issue his hesitancy was a manifestation of uncertainty about what, if any, U.S. interest mandated the use—and perhaps the loss—of U.S. troops. Some Europeans may have viewed this as weak-kneed dithering, but Clinton knew that being cautious was the only sensible course as a matter of domestic politics. Post–Cold War Europe is important to the United States, but just how important has yet to be determined by policy makers and by voters.

Since World War II, U.S. links to Europe have been the groundwork of foreign policy for parties on both sides of the Atlantic. Henry Kissinger has written that "the founders of the Atlantic ties—Truman, Acheson, Marshall, and Eisenhower—shared most Americans' reservations about the European style of diplomacy. But they understood that, without its Atlantic ties, America would find itself in a world of nations with which—except in the Western hemisphere—it has few moral bonds or common traditions." Kissinger also observed that "the great achievement of the postwar generation of American and European leaders was their recognition that, unless America was organically involved in Europe, it would be obliged to involve itself later under circumstances far less favorable to both sides of the Atlantic. That is even more true today. Germany has become so strong that existing European institutions cannot by themselves strike a balance between Germany and its European partners."[5] A similar sentiment was expressed by Raymond Seitz, U.S. ambassador to Great Britain from 1991 to 1994: "This vague thing called 'the American presence' is so important for Europe. It siphons off the poisons and anxieties of European history."[6]

The scope of future American activism remains in doubt. Great Britain's ambassador to the United States, John Kerr, in a speech in late 1996, said that looking ten years ahead, he expected that the United States would possess "a willingness to intervene in situations abroad, not just when a vital U.S. national interest is at stake, but when the values for which America stands are in some way being attacked or impugned."[7] That ascribes a noble idealism to the United States, but that kind of interventionism could prove disastrous for the U.S. politician who tried to make it operative policy.

U.S. reluctance about intervention is based in part on its physical insularity. German foreign affairs analyst Michael Stürmer offered this theory about the effect of this insularity on U.S. policy decisions: "To thank God for the protection offered by two surrounding oceans against the tribulations of the rest of the world while wishing to make the world safe for democracy has been the fundamental ambivalence governing American foreign policy in the twentieth century."[8]

Michael Mandelbaum of Johns Hopkins University notes that "the purpose of the United States is to prevent a big war" and to serve as the offshore balance so no single power will dominate Europe.[9] This has been an integral part of U.S. foreign policy for half a century. Beatrice Heuser, a professor at King's College in London, notes that post–World War II European integration was "encouraged, indeed in part driven, by the U.S. desire to end the long history of fratricidal wars among Europeans, which by the twentieth century had developed the tendency to suck in the United States."[10]

European disorder exerts a gravitational pull that the United States has proved able to resist only temporarily. British policy makers continue to operate on the assumption that in dire times the United States can be counted on.

The potency of U.S. public opinion should not, however, be underestimated. It operates as at least a drag on—if not a barrier to—U.S. response to overseas crises. The British government recognized this in 1940 and tried to build pro-British sentiment that would help push the United States into the war. Today, keeping the United States committed to Europe may require similar stroking. The line between informing and meddling tends to blur, so care should be taken in any such public relations ventures. But to do nothing—to entrust the future wholly to the past and expect eventual American involvement during a crisis—would be risky.

NATO'S FUTURE

Beyond a philosophy governing when and when not to intervene, there must exist an appropriate mechanism through which the intervention would take place. In Europe, that mechanism has been and presumably will continue to be NATO. So far, the British and U.S. governments have been in agreement about the general future of NATO: expand it to absorb some (and eventually perhaps most) of the former Warsaw Pact states. That scheme glows with the self-assurance born of the Cold War triumph. Aspirants to the club are getting in line, led by Poland, Hungary, and the Czech Republic, whose admission was approved at the July 1997 Madrid summit. Russia protests, but merely in the way it now does most things: feebly. NATO's hegemony is apparently confirmed.

NATO certainly can do whatever it wants, but what does it want? That question ought to be answered soon, certainly before the United States devises a long-term strategic plan for its own role in Europe. Great

Britain and the other current NATO members apparently expect the United States to retain its position as a NATO principal, but without the Soviet Union in the picture, U.S. and Western European interests diverge. Samuel Huntington has written that "with the Cold War over, NATO has one central and compelling purpose: to insure that it remains over by preventing the reimposition of Russian political and military control in Central Europe."[11]

That mission seems reasonable, but NATO expansion does carry some risks and costs. Fueling nationalist fervor in Russia is an issue that has been too quickly dismissed. Creation of what Michael Mandelbaum has referred to as a "Weimar Russia"—isolated and resentful—would be intrinsically destabilizing. The danger is not that an insecure Russia would send its army rolling westward into the heart of Europe; it is not capable of mounting that kind of attack. The more likely manifestation of insecurity would be Russian moves against its nearest neighbors, such as Ukraine or the Baltic states. A conflict of this kind would lap against the boundaries of the new NATO, which then would have to decide whether to watch or act. Neither course is appealing.

Russian journalist Aleksei Pushkov, writing in the *New York Times*, warned that "more than anything else, the NATO expansion is reviving Russia's old suspicions of the United States. After Russia removed all its troops from Eastern Europe and the Baltics, it does not understand why NATO troops should come to take their place in those countries. Russia strongly believes that it has the right to become part of modern Europe. An enlarged NATO with no arrangement to give Russia an equal say on security issues is perceived as a negation of such a right, as an attempt to refuse it a real voice in European matters." Pushkov noted that progress in arms control would suffer if Russia felt insecure, and he said that the United States "risks confronting not necessarily an enemy but a runaway train moving with growing speed in an unpredictable direction."[12]

In addition to considering Russia's reaction, the process of integrating new members needs much debate. John Major said in 1996 that "every new country joining NATO means a huge new commitment on their part and on the part of NATO. It is a military alliance, not a debating society. It will certainly not be a free lunch."[13]

Not only is the lunch not free, its price is beyond what NATO's potential new members can pay. According to the Congressional Budget Office, bringing the armed forces of these nations up to NATO standards may cost $125 billion during the next fifteen years. The Clinton White House has put the cost closer to $30 billion. Whatever the dollar amount, this is a post–Cold War expense that the U.S. Congress may be unwilling to take on. It may be true that to the victor belong the bills, but political support for paying those bills, especially after the initial delight in victory has faded, might be hard to find.

Despite these costs, Western European NATO members find expansion of the organization appealing in part because it would be less disruptive than bringing Eastern European states into the European Union. A reasonable fear exists that the "poor cousins" from the East would be an enormous drag on the EU's prosperity. The incremental costs of German reunification validate this concern.

These matters lead to the larger question: What exactly should the new NATO's mission be? When the North Atlantic Treaty was signed in 1949, the key provision provided that among the parties, "an armed attack against one or more of them . . . shall be considered an attack against them all," and they agreed that in such an event each signatory would take "such action as it deems necessary," including "the use of armed force, to restore and maintain the security of the North Atlantic area." This was a straightforward warning to the Soviet Union, and this was why NATO had been created.

Princeton University professor Richard Ullman has observed that NATO's "very success creates the conditions of its growing irrelevance, and therefore of its atrophy."[14] With the Soviet threat removed, NATO needs to define a new rationale for itself and consider the implications of that "attack against them all" clause. Should, for example, a border clash between Hungary (as a NATO member) and Croatia trigger a full NATO response? At the very least, NATO's charter could incorporate a dispute-arbitration clause, mandating binding arbitration and a suspension of disputants from mutual defense protection until the controversy is peacefully settled. In the United States, Senator Kay Bailey Hutchison has been among those urging this reform, which is the kind of condition the United States may want to see attached to its continuing commitment to NATO.

The organization's confused performance in dealing with the unraveling of the Balkans shows that much remains to be done to define the scope and mechanics of NATO operations. Impetus for this redefinition should come from the United States and Great Britain. For most of NATO's existence, these two countries have provided collegial leadership, presenting the Soviets with an alliance that despite its occasional fractiousness was fundamentally steadfast. Now these same two states are the logical leaders of the debate about the organization's future.

Reluctance to redefine NATO's mission stems in part from general satisfaction with its performance, but the context in which NATO will now exist has changed. The organization's European members appear quite comfortable with their relatively narrow responsibilities. RAND's Ronald Asmus writes: "While Europe's economic and commercial horizon is increasingly global, its strategic outlook remains regional. One of the ironies of history is that Europe's strategic mindset is narrower and more insular now than it was at the beginning of the twentieth century."[15] Countries such as Great Britain and France, which 100 years ago had colonies around the globe, now have little such possessory interest beyond Europe.

That insular outlook expands when issues such as the Middle East's oil supply are involved. Among the NATO issues to be considered, therefore, is a prospective "double enlargement." In addition to adding members, NATO might expand its mission to include non-European areas and issues that NATO members see as affecting their vital interests.[16] Margaret Thatcher has said that NATO must be prepared to act farther afield than had been foreseen at the time of its creation. The Gulf War, she observed, demonstrated "that NATO forces must be able to operate 'out of area.' The range of potential serious threats is now truly global. That does not mean that NATO forces should be deployed whenever some local crisis in a far-flung country occurs. But it does mean that major regional threats must concern us."[17]

Along the same lines, RAND's James Thomson writes:

> The United States and Europe share a clear interest in ensuring access to Persian Gulf oil at reasonable prices and in preventing the spread of nuclear weapons, especially in regions near Europe. . . . Taking a longer view, American-European mutual security interests are truly global. Owing to the importance of Pacific trade to the United States, and the rapid growth of East Asian economies, U.S. security interests in these regions are looming ever larger. But the same can be said for Europe because of its growing connections to Asian economic growth.

To protect those interests, suggests Thomson, NATO might add a new major command to its structure to deal with out-of-area contingencies.[18]

Some of the caution about enlarging NATO's mission stems from concern about overreaching. Former Secretary of Defense Dick Cheney says that the NATO countries other than the United States "haven't got very much capability to use outside their borders. There's a lot of bold talk, but the ability to project power for great distances is very limited for our European allies." He cites the Gulf War as an example of the NATO members' limitations, noting their reliance on the United States to provide them with comprehensive logistical support. Cheney suggests not formally redefining the NATO mission, but rather dealing with crises on an ad hoc basis. The United States could ask for help and probably receive it, he says, "but it's difficult to prewire."[19]

At the very least, some fine-tuning of NATO is in order. Maintaining the status quo may seem to be the easiest course to follow, but it will prove increasingly unrealistic. U.S. and British political leaders are the logical instigators of reform, and working together should prove more effective than operating individually. With similar worldviews, the United States and Great Britain should be able to define a coherent vision for NATO's future. One incentive is that if the United States and Great Britain fail to take the initiative, a Franco-German proposal may emerge. That could turn out to be perfectly acceptable, but leadership shifts on such important matters should not occur by default.

ANGLO-AMERICAN MILITARY COOPERATION

Policy makers in Washington and London also might consider developing separate and joint guidelines about intervention beyond the scope of NATO'S mandate. Despite Ambassador Kerr's prognostication about an activist United States, political realism is likely to dampen American officials' ardor for military intervention (except when "intervention" can be undertaken from a safe distance, as with cruise missiles).

Even a continuation of diplomatic activism by the United States should not be assumed. Endeavors such as Middle East shuttle negotiating have become hallmarks of recent American administrations, but this is more crisis management than foreign policy. It depends principally on the whim of the president and in some ways is merely a nostalgic display of putative clout, not part of a grand leadership scheme.

These expeditions—sometimes quixotic, sometimes realistic—are primarily free-lance ventures, with allies informed (perhaps) but not often invited to become truly involved. The real need for allied cooperation arises mainly on the rare occasion when a major military action is in the works, as in the Persian Gulf in 1990–91. The U.S.-British partnership in this case operated smoothly; both countries had a vital interest in keeping Middle East oil reserves out of Iraq's hands.

This was a classic rationale for going to war. The stakes were such that being too cautious could have proved disastrous. Blasting Saddam Hussein out of Kuwait was one thing; dislodging him from Saudi Arabia without massive destruction in the oil fields would have been a very different task. Great Britain, under Margaret Thatcher and then John Major, was prompt and unflinching in support of the Bush administration's tough line toward Iraq and the U.S. efforts to build consensus and create a diverse military coalition.

The Gulf War also underscored Great Britain's status as the most competent military ally of the United States. Laurence Martin, former director of the Royal Institute of International Affairs, said that in this war, "all of a sudden the British counted again."[20]

Douglas Hurd, who was British foreign secretary during the war, appraises British strength this way: "We're a military power—not a great military power but a good military power. We have a global view of the world. We're willing to participate. The one superpower cannot do everything on its own. . . . We are a medium-sized nation with some very good troops. They don't make us preeminent, but they make us interesting."[21] On other occasions, Hurd has noted that "we punch above our weight."

Former U.S. defense secretary Dick Cheney agrees: "The Brits are good." He adds, "It's easier for us to work with the Brits than just about anybody else" because of the history of the partnership, the common language, and similar military doctrine.[22]

The Gulf War is pointed to as proof that the Anglo-American alliance is intact and effective, but this may have been the exception rather than the rule. Iraq's behavior was so egregious and the stakes—the oil reserves—were so high that taking firm action was virtually unavoidable. That kind of clear-cut situation is rare. The more common scenario may turn out to be one such as unfolded in the Balkans, where the fighting had enough ripple effects in Europe to make it in Great Britain's interest to do something, but was distant enough from the United States (except when television brought gory scenes into American living rooms) to make activism problematic.

Laurence Martin asks an important question: "Will the United States really participate in peacekeeping operations on a regular basis, will it be a true partner, or will it rather pursue a course of 'erratic dominance'?"[23] In the former Yugoslavia, says Douglas Hurd, "It was very unattractive for the Europeans to be acting on the ground while the United States was standing on the sideline. It was very irksome. We were taking the risks and getting the blame."[24] From the American standpoint, however, the Balkans war illustrated that there can be European defense issues that are not perceived as "Atlantic issues" by the United States. Former U.S. ambassador to Great Britain Raymond Seitz notes that "there is no longer a seamless security interest" such as had existed during the Cold War.[25]

Although a sense of NATO-based responsibility, however incompletely defined, tugged at the United States in the Balkans case, more remote conflicts will provide more severe tests of U.S. and British responsiveness, separate and joint. In Rwanda, for example, the case for intervention was based solely on humanitarian concerns; an internecine war in central Africa posed no threat to U.S. or British interests. In such a case, should the United States or Great Britain act, either on its own or under United Nations auspices? If the United States responds on its own initiative, can it count on Britain and other NATO members to help? The easy answer is to defer to the United Nations, but sometimes the United Nations moves slowly, ineptly, or not at all. Even if the United Nations does call for a response, to what extent should the United States and Great Britain take the lead in answering that call?

British foreign secretary Robin Cook has raised an ethical question related to such matters: "We are instant witness in our sitting rooms through the medium of television to human tragedy in distant lands, and are therefore obliged to accept moral responsibility for our response."[26] The extent to which this responsibility affects policy is yet to be seen.

Raymond Seitz offers a word of caution about such matters, noting that "there are some issues in which you don't want the Americans involved because that immediately escalates the situation."[27] If there are three levels of crisis, strategic, midlevel, and police, it may be that true U.S. involvement should be limited to the first, perhaps providing logistical support in the other two categories to parties more directly concerned. The United States may want to remain above the fray in most cases, a loftiness appropriate to a superpower. Rather than being a party to every dispute, the United States might want to be seen as an ultimate arbitrator, on the theory that "superpowers don't do windows."

For its part, Great Britain also faces the task of defining guidelines for intervention, whether it acts on its own, with the United States, or in a larger partnership. Particularly if the United States appears reluctant to respond to European crises, Great Britain will be looked to as a leader, but others may want to assert themselves.

If doubts arise in Europe about U.S. reliability, a reordering of the power structure will certainly occur. Despite French pretensions, the only real candidates for leadership are Great Britain and Germany. No one is eager to see military-related competition between these two countries.

The best way to avoid it is to keep the United States actively participating, and the best way for that to happen is for the British to continue to make the case to the Americans that the future of the United States cannot be divorced from the future of Europe. In both countries, politicians extol this, but when the rhetoric must be turned into policy, enthusiasm is sometimes lost.

HONG KONG

In some cases, the U.S. partnership with Great Britain may make U.S. involvement more likely. Although as of July 1997, Hong Kong was turned over by Great Britain to China, British interest in its former colony will remain high. If the Chinese government should renege on its pledges of careful treatment of Hong Kong and impose the repressive measures that the rest of China endures, Britain is sure to protest angrily and look for ways to retaliate. The specifics of such a response are uncertain, but without doubt Britain will be counting on its allies, especially the United States, for firm support.

Firmness, however, is not a characteristic of most U.S. policy toward China. Whenever U.S. officials are tempted to criticize the Chinese about their trade practices or their less-than-enlightened attitudes about human rights, visions of the riches waiting to be mined from the vast Chinese market suddenly come into focus. After a brief tut-tutting, business as usual resumes; the Chinese do whatever they want, and the Americans dream about selling trillions of cigarettes to coughing Chinese and building a Disneyland near Shanghai. But if Hong Kong is victimized, Britain is unlikely to tolerate mushiness from its friends. Therefore, the Hong Kong transition period will prove to be an important test not just of Chinese intentions but also of the solidity of the U.S.-British relationship.

The departure from Hong Kong is the final step in the dissolution of the British Empire. Hong Kong was acquired "in perpetuity" as part of the 1842 Treaty of Nanking. (The Jingansi temple where the humiliating terms of the treaty were imposed on China has been turned into a museum with exhibits about the evils of British imperialism.) The treaty was renegotiated in 1898, transforming the outright grant into a ninety-nine-year lease. In 1984, Margaret Thatcher and Premier Zhao Ziyang signed a joint declaration about the 1997 transfer. China's National People's Congress approved a "Basic Law" for Hong Kong, adopting the concept of "one country, two systems" as the basis for the integration of the colony into China. Although Britain attempted to institute some last-minute human rights guarantees and claimed the right to monitor the status of such freedoms and to be consulted about governance after the transition, the Chinese quickly made it clear that Britain would have no residual rights at all.

Fearing a flood of Hong Kong immigrants, Britain granted some Hong Kong residents full citizenship rights while leaving millions more with passports that allow them to come to Britain without a visa but not to live there. Of course, if the situation in Hong Kong deteriorates, these "visitors" might arrive with no intention of returning to Asia. That is one of the reasons Britain has moved so carefully in its dealings with China, trying to keep fearfulness out of the transition.

The United States has a considerable stake itself in Hong Kong: more than $12 billion in direct investment; more than 40,000 American citizens living there; and about 1,000 American businesses represented there, employing 250,000 people (according to the American Chamber of Commerce), which is about 10 percent of the Hong Kong work force. Emerging from the inconsistencies of U.S. China policy is the United States–Hong Kong Policy Act, passed by Congress in 1992 and reaffirmed in 1996, which provides the kind of support the British want. The act declares that after the transfer of power, the United States should "continue to treat Hong Kong as a separate territory in economic and trade matters," one that is "fully autonomous from the People's Republic of China." This act, which is nonbinding, also opens the way for the president to seek punitive measures against China if Hong Kong's social and economic systems are not preserved. Among the steps the United States might take against China would be suspension of Hong Kong's own most-favored-nation trading status.[28]

Of course, China is no more likely to give ground to the United States than to Great Britain. The official Chinese policy is that Hong Kong has become an internal matter. If Washington acts "provocatively" about this issue, China might respond in kind about matters such as its weapons exports and even adherence to nuclear-nonproliferation agreements.

Most British officials speak very carefully and quietly about the potential for a major Hong Kong crisis. They recognize that the United Nations would not act; China's Security Council veto would see to that. Meaningful trade sanctions also would be hard to devise and enforce. The option cited by some British officials (but not for attribution) is "a common Western response" to let China know that "its behavior will affect the speed at which it is incorporated into the global system." Without something more specific, China, given its actions in recent years, may not be impressed.

All this means that U.S. support for Great Britain on Hong Kong is extremely important. But it also is intrinsically high-risk, with unpleasant outcomes much more likely than positive ones. As Hong Kong passed from British to Chinese rule, U.S. policy makers offered one of their periodic displays of resolve, talking tough about the need to maintain Hong Kong residents' rights. The British recognized this and were appreciative, particularly because their European allies had not been as supportive as had the Americans. Christopher Lockwood, diplomatic editor of the *Daily Telegraph*, wrote in April 1997 that "if freedom survives in Hong Kong after the Great Chinese Takeaway, it will do so thanks to America, and not to Britain or Europe." Citing President Clinton's meeting with Martin Lee, Hong Kong's most prominent liberal, and the president's warning to China that Hong Kong's freedoms must be protected, Lockwood wrote: "One might have hoped that it would be Europe taking the lead on Hong Kong. . . . What better way to show that Europe is the coming economic superpower with a global diplomacy to match?" But, he noted, countries such as France were more interested in preserving their own business deals with the Chinese and so were not interested in provoking Beijing.[29]

During his visit to London in May 1997, Clinton took the occasion of a joint news conference with Prime Minister Blair to underscore the U.S. commitment to Hong Kong: "We will keep faith with the people of Hong Kong by monitoring the transition to make sure that its civil liberties are maintained. Those are the things for which the United Kingdom and the United States stand, and those are the things that the [1984] agreement guarantees."[30] Members of Britain's foreign policy establishment privately expressed their approval of Washington's increasingly tough stance. Some attributed the ascendance of hard-liners to the Clinton administration's desire to show that its Asia policy had not been improperly influenced by campaign contributions, but the most common sentiment was that the United States was simply looking after itself. Noting the massive U.S. financial presence in Hong Kong, former Foreign Secretary Douglas Hurd said, "It is in the U.S.'s interest that Hong Kong continue to thrive."[31] Presumably a response to severe Chinese misbehavior would be based on trade sanctions, but Asia's volatility means that any policy, particularly a punitive one, should be implemented with extraordinary care.

The reaction from Britain and Hong Kong to U.S. expressions of concern has been appreciative but sometimes also cautious. Fears of U.S. overreaction have led some Hong Kong business and political leaders to tell Washington not to worry too much about the former colony's future. They point out that any U.S. harshness toward China would also hurt Hong Kong.

The consensus emerging soon after the 1997 turnover was that policy toward Hong Kong should be based on the assumption that Hong Kong can take care of itself. The uncertainty about China's plans for Hong Kong makes understandable the pendulum-like swings of U.S. and, to a lesser extent, British thinking about what to do next. Presumably, any U.S. initiatives related to Hong Kong would be undertaken only after consultation with Britain. On this issue, it would make little sense for the United States and Great Britain to follow separate paths.

Throughout Asia, populations, economic prowess, and military strength are growing. Great Britain and the United States are not mere bystanders; Britain has past and present Commonwealth members there, and the United States has defense and economic commitments throughout the region. So far, the U.S. and British strategy for Asia seems to be "keep the lid on and make as much money as possible." Perhaps that is the essence of sound foreign policy.

NUCLEAR WEAPONS AND CONVENTIONAL FORCES

In Asia, as elsewhere, the United States and Great Britain have similar and sometimes shared interests. During the Cold War, defense of these interests around the world was based on a variety of strategic ploys and ultimately on the West's nuclear arsenal. The unquestioned ability of the United States and the Soviet Union to decimate the planet was never far from the minds of those who made policy and those who enjoyed or suffered its consequences.

During the 1950s, the United States gave substance to the special relationship by providing a unique supply of information and material that greatly aided the British in developing their own nuclear-weapons program. In 1962, President John Kennedy agreed to sell Britain Polaris missiles. Although Britain's independent nuclear deterrent has always been subsidiary to American weaponry, it has been an important issue in British politics as well as in allied defense strategy. During the 1980s, the Conservative and Labour parties fiercely debated Britain's nuclear role. Labour party official Denis Healey was a member of a delegation to Moscow in 1986 to whom Mikhail Gorbachev "gave a firm pledge that if Britain gave up its nuclear weapons, the Soviet Union would dismantle the equivalent number of its own."[32]

For her part, Margaret Thatcher denounced Labour party leader Neil Kinnock because his party had called for a nonnuclear defense policy, including closure of U.S. nuclear bases in Britain. "Mr. Kinnock," she wrote, "had also made it clear that there were no circumstances in which he would ask the United States to use nuclear weapons in the defense of Britain." This meant, she continued, that under a Labour government, "Britain would be regarded by the Soviets as no longer under the American and NATO 'nuclear umbrella,' " which would leave the British intolerably vulnerable.[33]

As the 1990s draw to a close, Great Britain and the United States must decide how many nuclear weapons they need. Assuming that the warheads cached in various places in the former Soviet Union can be accounted for, the principal nuclear menace that existed since the end of World War II will be gone, at least for now. But despite treaties and detective work, the proliferation of nuclear weapons is certain to continue, some of it detected, some of it not. A hitherto unthreatening nation or unheard-of terrorist group coming into possession of one or more of these weapons is not just the stuff of Tom Clancy novels. Great Britain and the United States must consider how they would try to prevent being attacked and how they would answer if they were attacked. Choice of response is not as self-evident as it was when—in Barry Goldwater's phrase—"lobbing one into the men's room of the Kremlin" may have seemed an appropriate option.

The nature of such military threats demands a redefinition of the Cold War concept of deterrence. Perhaps most logical now, at least in terms of dealing with major powers, is "minimum deterrence": retain enough strategic nuclear weapons to have a second-strike capability.[34] Having a huge nuclear arsenal might once have checked reckless action by a major power, but it is unlikely to divert a small, outlaw state or group intent on wreaking havoc. It may be that the most effective military tools now are aircraft and tactical missiles, plus Delta Force or Special Air Services teams, that can deliver precise, controlled blows.

The technology of warfare is changing rapidly in ways that should reinforce U.S. superiority. For instance, the U.S. military is far ahead of any other country's armed forces in linking information technology to weaponry. A leader in *The Economist* in March 1997 raised some of the issues these changes affect: the revolution in military technology, "by increasing American might, may encourage the country's unilateralist element to think it can win wars without having to work with troublesome partners." But, said the article, the United States might share some of its new technologies, both to help allies be more self-reliant and to save money by aiding allies and then sending them a bill. This might also change U.S. policy about sending U.S. personnel into action: "When America wants to intervene abroad it may expect its allies to provide troops but offer high-tech equipment as a quid pro quo." Europe, said *The Economist*, "may not like the idea of an alliance even more dominated by the United States, but . . . better a dominant than a unilateralist America."[35]

Budget as well as strategic issues will shape decisions about how much military capability, nuclear and conventional, is necessary today. Great Britain and the United States are reducing the size of their armed forces. Since 1989, the U.S. armed forces have shrunk from 2,163,200 to about 1,500,000. In Europe, U.S. troop strength declined from 317,000 in 1989 toward the eventual target of 100,000. Britain's reductions are as follows[36]:

	1990	1997
Defense budget (billions of pounds; 1997 prices)	26.4	21.1
Strength of forces (thousands)	315	215
Infantry battalions	55	40
Conventionally armed submarines	28	12
Frigates/destroyers	48	35
Front-line tanks	699	304
Front-line fighters and bombers	630	500

Pounds are measured in U.S. billions (a thousand millions).

Anglo-American teamwork can help avoid duplication of effort, and by sharing intelligence wiser judgments can be made about what levels of forces are needed and where they should be deployed. The accepted Pentagon wisdom of the moment is that the United States should be able to fight two serious conventional wars simultaneously. An essential part of that theory is reliance on allies, both collectively, as in NATO, and individually.

As a matter of U.S. domestic politics, such sharing of the load is essential. In the past, support could be found, although sometimes with difficulty, for substantial defense-budget outlays to counter the Soviets, especially in Europe. Now, with so much pressure on U.S. politicians to balance the national budget, eliminate the long-running deficit, and re-order spending priorities, defense expenditures generally, and spending for the defense of Europe in particular, require different rationales.

This kind of restructuring does not mean that the United States is looking for a way out of Europe. Dick Cheney is among those who believe that a strong U.S. presence remains vital to European security. That means, he says, "military force on the ground." Noting that "the Euro-peans are not capable of overcoming their divisions" when it comes to forging a unified defense policy, he says that the U.S. role is that of "the anchor of effective security. The U.S. is the one that has to provide the leadership."[37]

Great Britain and other allies must decide how much money, person-nel, and equipment they will provide. In doing so, they could alter the essence of the alliance, and U.S. dominance might decrease. This will not reach the point at which the United States becomes a secondary player, but realignment of responsibility logically brings with it a realign-ment of authority.

This change in relationships will occur even with the across-the-board diminution of military capabilities. The issue for Great Britain and for other major powers is a matter of scale: do they want to do more than fill in the gaps left by U.S. downsizing? Might Great Britain, France, Ger-many, Japan, or some other country decide to recast its defense philosophy in a way that makes it more independently formidable, such as by building new weapons systems? Will these states ever consider independent nuclear-weapons development?

As the Cold War proved, expanding military clout means incurring massive debt. It is hard to imagine any major power being willing now to align economic priorities in such a defense-oriented way. For one thing, the domestic political price for doing so would probably be unsustainable.

Governance of a redesigned shared defense capability will be compli-cated. Former British ambassador to the United States Robin Renwick has noted that "even more than monetary union, an effective common defense policy would require unified central control. It would also require a large increase in defense budgets to give a European entity the sea, airlift, and real-time intelligence capabilities that at present are lack-ing."[38]

The two principal testing grounds for any such changes will be Europe and Asia, both volatile and both accustomed to the stabilizing presence of the United States. Before any country alters political and military equilibrium, the purpose and cost of doing so should be clear. For instance, any pulling back from NATO by the United States will create a vacuum that might be filled by Germany. Aftershocks from such changes would certainly be felt: in Europe, Russia would look suspiciously on any Western military upgrading, especially by Germany. In Asia, if the United States were to pull back, China and others would watch warily for any change in Japanese military policy. This is all speculative, but with so many aspects of geopolitics in flux, it makes sense to speculate. The case for U.S. involvement—at the very least as a defender of last resort—remains compelling.

In Great Britain, the Blair government shows no inclination to go it alone. Significantly expanding Britain's defense capability makes no sense, strategically or fiscally. It is important from Britain's standpoint to make certain that U.S. downsizing not go beyond a certain point. Britain's reliance on the United States has changed but not evaporated since the Cold War ended.

SUSTAINING PEACE IN EUROPE

British participation in the Persian Gulf War proved the adequacy of the nation's response to a major crisis. It is hard to foresee any larger military event that Great Britain would have to handle without being able to count on substantial assistance from the United States. During the next few years, the United States, Britain, and other nations will be devising the formulae they need for retaining appropriate post–Cold War military preparedness. That should be a collegial process, especially between the United States and Britain. It may produce significant budget savings for both, and, more important, it may improve the chances of sustaining peace.

For this to happen, however, the United States and Great Britain, as well as NATO collectively, must more precisely define their goals. As an objective, "keeping the peace" is too vague. If "peace" refers to a more or less amicable coexistence among the major powers, it may be achievable, but if it means the absence of war more generally, it is probably illusory for two reasons: someone, somewhere, will always be fighting; and putting a halt to any fighting requires the will as well as the ability to do so. Attempts to bring peace to the former Yugoslavia during the early

1990s underscored how difficult it can be to summon political resolve and combine it with military competence.

This is a critical matter for the United States and Great Britain because if they cannot act in concert, it is unlikely that a larger alliance will be able to do so. Just as these countries must decide what constitutes a vital interest worth fighting for, so too must they determine how regional peacekeeping should work. In the Balkans, the trial-and-error approach to these issues allowed ethnic cleansing and other abominations to continue far too long. The United States, in particular, must come to understand the moral flaws inherent in wanting power without responsibility and the pragmatic difficulties that can be created by inaction. Sir Robin Renwick cites events in Bosnia as evidence that "the exercise of power requires real unity of purpose and the ability to make credible military threats." He notes that only when the United States participated aggressively was an agreement between the warring parties attained.[39]

Beyond defining a political philosophy that is both morally and pragmatically sound, the mechanics of restoring and keeping peace need to be better established. Leadership from the United States and Great Britain could help create, for example, a policing authority to enforce international justice standards, such as by pursuing people convicted of war crimes. It is not that this is particularly the business of these two nations, but someone must display initiative, and who is more likely to do so than they?

Questions about leadership will become more common, especially if the United States proves hesitant about continuing in the role it assumed after World War II. Inertia easily takes hold, particularly when forging common military policy is the task at hand. This topic can always reignite smoldering resentments among nations. The United States and Great Britain seem to do better than most at avoiding that trap.

To some in Europe, however, this pairing may appear inappropriate given the growing emphasis on multilateral over bilateral action. The French are particularly sensitive about being cut out of the action. But the need for a certain comfort level in the most important relationships means that Anglo-American closeness will continue. From that affinity may come the impetus needed to push decision making forward, which is something that might become increasingly valued in the professedly egalitarian new Europe.

Structuring this relationship may be tricky, because despite the value of their bilateral cooperation, neither the United States nor Great Britain wants to move too far outside the larger community. The task, then, is to fine-tune the long-standing partnership to ensure the continued capability of mounting joint military operations (a compatibility that already exists within the NATO system) and intelligence sharing. Teamwork in this latter field is always complicated by the proprietary nature of the business and well-founded fears about the adequacy of security in both nations' intelligence agencies.

The Anglo-American intelligence partnership has been often colorful and mostly successful. In 1940, British intelligence chief Stewart Menzies assigned Canadian William Stephenson to New York to gather information about enemy activity in the Western Hemisphere and to build bridges between the British and U.S. intelligence communities. (The latter did not amount to much at the time.) Stephenson worked closely with "Wild Bill" Donovan, who became the first head of the Office of Strategic Services (OSS), the predecessor of the Central Intelligence Agency (CIA). Donovan was a persistent advocate for the British cause, and during World War II the OSS worked effectively with Britain's Secret Intelligence Service (SIS).

The postwar partnership encompassed adventures and misadventures, such as overthrowing Iran's Mossadegh government and trying to penetrate Albania. Links between the CIA and SIS (also known as MI-6) were damaged in the 1960s by the revelation that Kim Philby, who had been the SIS's Washington liaison officer, and some other SIS operatives were Soviet agents. Mistrust persisted, although usually at a manageable level, with intelligence bosses in London and Washington wary of their counterpart agencies but nonetheless recognizing that they had to keep working together.

One of the more useful cooperative ventures has been the UKUSA Agreement, which was crafted in 1947 to create a comprehensive plan for gathering signals (communications) intelligence. The United States, Great Britain, Canada, Australia, and New Zealand are the principals, carving up the world into zones of responsibility. Christopher Andrew, in his history of the British secret service, writes: "During the war, Britain had been the senior partner in the intelligence alliance. The UKUSA pact was to turn her into the junior partner. . . . America's wealth gave her, for the first time, the intelligence as well as the military leadership of the Western world."[40]

The United States and Great Britain continue to share intelligence duties, such as monitoring public radio broadcasts from around the world to glean information about the source countries' domestic politics. Also,

U.S. photo-reconnaissance aircraft sometimes use British bases, such as those in Cyprus to keep watch on the Middle East. During the Falklands War, U.S. SR-71 spy planes flew over Argentina, and the Reagan administration gave the photographs to the British.

This facet of the Anglo-American partnership is also still evolving. Dick Cheney says that "the task of intelligence has changed to some extent." For example, terrorism, he says, "doesn't lend itself to the technical solutions [such as satellite surveillance] we used to keep track of the Soviet order of battle." Cheney also notes the strains on Anglo-American intelligence cooperation created by the Soviet penetration of the U.S. intelligence community, as in the Aldrich Ames case, which Cheney calls "devastating."[41]

Nevertheless, Anglo-American cooperation in this field continues as a matter of course. Despite its complexities, intelligence remains a logical area in which the "specialness" of the Anglo-American relationship can continue to be put to work. William Crowe, former chairman of the Joint Chiefs of Staff and U.S. ambassador to Britain from 1994 to 1997, says that Anglo-American intelligence ties "are so close they couldn't be severed even if we wanted to."[42]

THE WESTERN EUROPEAN UNION

In almost all of these defense-related matters, substantial questions remain about obligations to multilateral bodies, principally the United Nations, NATO, and—for Great Britain but not the United States—the Western European Union (WEU). In the declarations attached to the Maastricht Treaty, Declaration 30 addressed the WEU: "WEU will be developed as the defense component of the European Union and as a means to strengthen the European pillar of the Atlantic Alliance [NATO]. To this end, it will formulate common European defense policy and carry forward its concrete implementation through the further development of its own operational role." This statement is nicely vague, putting the EU on record in support of having its own common defense policy—without a transatlantic component—but not calling for the WEU to supersede NATO.

Numerous concerns exist about duplication of effort, divided loyalties, and complexities of command structure. As the memberships of NATO and the European Union grow, expanded cooperation between the WEU and NATO will be increasingly logical, if not increasingly simple. With NATO's mission changed since its Cold War days, its role is somewhat like that of the WEU. In any discussions about respective roles for NATO and the WEU, U.S. participation is always an important topic, whether explicit or implicit in the talks.

British officials see the WEU now as a vehicle for humanitarian, rescue, and low-level peace-enforcement efforts. They profess interest in building up European military capability, but they recognize, as one British military official put it, that "the WEU is not yet mature enough to handle crises." He added, "From our perspective it is terribly important to keep the U.S. involved in Europe."

That view is not universally shared. There is, as always, some resentment about dependence on the United States. British scholar William Wallace writes, "There has been an irritating undertone of imperial hegemony in the American approach, with arguments that the United States must ensure that NATO, rather than the EU, defines the structure and boundaries of a wider Europe, while insisting that the European allies must shoulder the consequent costs." But the blame, says Wallace, should not be placed entirely on the United States:

> We also have to recognize that it has been partly the incapacity and indirection of West European governments which left the U.S. administration to lead, and allowed NATO enlargement in effect to displace EU enlargement in reshaping European international politics. West European governments now have no choice but to attempt to ensure that the two processes reinforce each other rather than inflame transatlantic tensions and alarm East Europeans.[43]

Regardless of accusations of "imperial hegemony," fundamental U.S. policy remains based on the preservation of NATO. In 1990, France, Germany, and Italy proposed that the WEU should become an integral part of the EU, as its defense arm. The Bush administration responded with stern warnings against doing anything that might undermine NATO. The following year, Helmut Kohl and François Mitterand modified the plan, suggesting that the WEU become the defense mechanism of the EU but with membership limited to NATO members.[44] This was the concept of the WEU as the European pillar of NATO that was incorporated in the declarations accompanying the 1992 Maastricht Treaty. (Not all European members of NATO belong to the EU, and not all EU members belong to NATO.)

The United States continues to watch the WEU warily, particularly as it moves toward its stated ideal of becoming *the* unified European defense entity. U.S. ambassador to Britain William Crowe said in 1996: "Washington remains an interested observer as EU member states discuss greater foreign policy and/or security cooperation. These decisions, of course, are for the European players to sort out. But the U.S. has a strong interest in preserving the foreign policy flexibility and responsiveness which we currently enjoy in the bilateral relationships with our allies."[45] Similarly, Dick Cheney says that although "the U.S. cannot stand in the way" of an independent European force, "I'd be careful about it."[46]

Some British foreign policy experts share the U.S. concerns about the WEU. Charles Powell, national security adviser to Prime Ministers Thatcher and Major, cautions against creation of any European defense force, saying, "It's a great mistake to detract in any way from NATO." Powell says that undercutting NATO would encourage the United States to back away from Europe and would advance the idea of a federal Europe. He also makes the point that U.S. help, at least with logistics such as airlift capability, is essential in any significant military operation.[47]

Foreign Secretary Robin Cook addressed these questions soon after the 1997 British elections, making clear that Great Britain would not endorse a policy that might undercut NATO: "We want to develop a European security and defense identity. We see that primarily being done within NATO."[48] The following month, Prime Minister Blair also spoke of the issue after returning from the Amsterdam meeting of the EU's European Council: "Getting Europe's voice heard more clearly in the world will not be achieved through merging the EU and WEU or developing an unrealistic common defense policy. We therefore resisted unacceptable proposals from others. Instead, we argued for—and won—the explicit recognition, written into the Treaty [governing the EU] for the first time, that NATO is the foundation of our and other allies' common defense."[49] This is also the basic U.S. view. With the United States and Great Britain coordinating their political efforts on this matter, their joint position is likely to dominate the debate and determine its outcome.

In the search for middle ground, the plan for the Combined Joint Task Forces (CJTF) was created. The concept originally arose as a way for France to send troops into the Balkans without putting them under NATO command. The CJTF would be "separable" from NATO military command but not a permanent part of the WEU.[50] In practice, the CJTF is not really a step toward an independent European defense entity because it is a NATO subsidiary, dependent on NATO—meaning U.S.—logistical support.

At the 1997 Madrid summit, the NATO-WEU linkage took more

definite shape with endorsement of a European Security and Defense Identity that is to exist within NATO and help make NATO assets available to the WEU.[51] Again, implicit in such a venture is reliance on U.S. support.

The status quo seems to be based on a right of first refusal for NATO, with the WEU or a CJTF acting in lieu of NATO only if the United States decides that this is the best course of action. This guarantee of NATO dominance has won the support of policy makers in both Washington and London.[52] Another factor that dampens enthusiasm about the WEU is the fear that it would be entangled in the ever-growing EU bureaucracy, which has a cumbersome decision-making process not well suited to crisis response. This brings to mind a question asked by Henry Kissinger and others: "When I want to talk to Europe, whom do I call?"

So far, the WEU has no troops except those it can borrow on an ad hoc basis. It has done so on several occasions, such as helping to enforce an arms embargo against the former Yugoslavia and providing a police force for the Bosnian city of Mostar. In 1997, when the EU wanted to "do something" about the chaos plaguing Albania, there was not much the WEU could offer. The EU's efforts at establishing a common security policy also suffer greatly from the absence of a planning process. In the Albanian case, for example, there was no EU mechanism to anticipate problems and plan accordingly. Instead, the EU's role was entirely reactive.

Despite continuing talk about a beefed-up WEU, the notion of a diminished U.S. role remains unappealing enough to deter significant movement toward a self-sufficient European defense mechanism. The German factor looms large in this. As long as the United States is the ultimate guarantor of European security, Germany is unlikely to feel threatened. Remove the U.S. shield, however, and Germany would certainly reassess its situation. Either Germany or one of the other Western European states might decide to establish itself as first among equals. Such a departure from the cozy status quo of the past fifty years could lead to the resurrection of old rivalries and tensions.

In 1995, British foreign secretary Malcolm Rifkind reiterated the case for unity in preserving European security. His premise was not far removed from that on which NATO had been founded nearly half a century before. "The classic concepts of the balance of power within Europe," he said, "have lost much of their relevance. There is no strategic threat to the safety of the United Kingdom that would not also be a similar threat to

France or to Germany. The interests that bind Europe together have become far greater than the interests that occasionally divide us."[53]

That emphasis on unity may be the official wisdom, but many of those who are skeptical about the new Europe warn of a decline in autonomy. Similar issues affect U.S. politics in terms of how U.S. forces fit into the United Nations military system and how NATO operations are to be directed. Despite much Wilsonian rhetoric about the desirability of multilateral cooperation, a greater feeling of security often exists between parties to bilateral military agreements. To some extent, the future of U.S.-British security ties will depend on the evolving attitudes about shared command and responsibility. When France, for example, insists that NATO's southern command be directed by a French officer rather than an American, U.S. officials are likely to feel greater fondness toward their British colleagues and toward simpler, two-nation policy formulation.

NEW ALIGNMENTS

A larger and more complex task involves trying to anticipate new alignments of friends and foes. For instance, Samuel Huntington advances this thesis about the "clash of civilizations": "In the post–Cold War world, the most important distinctions among peoples are not ideological, political, or economic. They are cultural." He points to "Muslim bellicosity" as an example of the new challenges the West must meet.[54]

Huntington's theory has its critics, but at the very least, it should stimulate some diplomatic preventive maintenance. Both the United States, with its history of paternalism toward other countries (especially those in the Western Hemisphere), and Great Britain, with its own imperialist tradition, may find it difficult to retool their attitudes about nations such as Brazil and Pakistan that may be much more powerful players in the twenty-first century than they have been in the past.

For the moment, the principal task is to maintain and simultaneously redefine U.S. attitudes about and the U.S. role in Europe. Michael Mandelbaum warns that

Europe could come to appear to Americans to be a large, wealthy, undeserving welfare case, indeed one whose own vitality has been sapped by its dependence on American protection. An American retreat from Europe is possible, finally, because it was the settled

policy of the United States before the Cold War to avoid engage-
ment in the politics of the continent in peacetime, and prior to
World War I to avoid entanglement in European affairs at any
time.[55]

Sir Robin Renwick also notes some fragility in the U.S. commitment
to Europe. He writes that a vital task for Great Britain is "to help ensure
that the United States is not left alone to respond to crises in which the
interests of the West generally are engaged." He cites the Persian Gulf
War as an example and adds that support for the United States is essential
because "protectionism and isolationism are recessive genes in the U.S.
body politic."[56]

A British military official offers a similar view: "Americans have a right
to expect us to play our part more robustly when events occur on Europe's
doorstep." He added that he believes that Britain and its European allies
are willing to do this and notes that British public opinion, more so than
U.S. opinion, tends to rally behind military action, even to the point of
accepting casualties as part of the price of wielding power. According to
Professor Beatrice Heuser,

> The question of reciprocity is something that any sensible U.S. gov-
> ernment will bring to the attention of the Europeans. It is time that
> the Europeans stopped behaving as net receivers of security, taking
> action only where their own interest is directly concerned. Any new
> transatlantic bargain should compel the Europeans to back the
> North Americans in their attempts to protect military stability in
> the Far East and elsewhere in the world. Given the EU's gross eco-
> nomic product compared with that of the United States, there is no
> excuse for European passivity.[57]

European members lag far behind the United States in paying for
NATO. In 1995, defense expenditures by European members totaled
about $165 billion, or 66 percent of the U.S. total. European spending
on defense research and development was about 35 percent of the U.S.
total, and on procurement it was about 70 percent of the U.S. outlay.[58]
With NATO's expansion, the United States is likely to find itself picking
up an even larger share of the tab.

Fine-tuning is certain to occur within the European defense community. Nevertheless, for the foreseeable future, the United States will remain the dominant military power in the world. Great Britain and other

U.S. allies need not fear being cast adrift, but given the rhetoric of frugality so popular now in American politics, financial burden sharing and other evidence of long-term self-sufficiency will be critical factors in determining how readily U.S. power will be made available when its allies need and want it.

The Anglo-American partnership remains the foundation on which European security is constructed. There is no reason for this not to continue. A peaceful Europe is in the interest of the United States; the insularity the Atlantic might seem to provide is largely illusory.

No other ally is as valuable as a coprotector of U.S. security. The British have displayed the competence and the willingness to play this role. As the new version of NATO takes shape, Great Britain is likely to support U.S. positions on enlargement of membership and mission. It is up to the United States, however, to make a compelling case for these changes. There is a tendency among Washington policy makers to issue edicts rather than build consensus. The Clinton administration is not alone in having done this, but its insensitivity about the nuances of alliance building may prove particularly damaging because of the uncertainty about NATO's future direction.

The Blair government has backed Clinton's 1997 expansion formula and has sided with the United States when France and, to a lesser extent, Germany have sought an expanded and more formalized European security role within or even beyond NATO. But no one will benefit in the long run from a schism between Anglo-American and Franco-German interests. To retain its maximum influence within Europe, Great Britain cannot be seen as being unduly in thrall to the United States. Americans should recognize this and work with the British to bridge gaps in the Atlantic alliance, and the British should nudge the Americans to make sure this happens.

For the most part, Churchill's vision of a grand strategic partnership has been fulfilled. It will not, however, be sustained by nostalgia. It needs continued attention from thoughtful leaders on both sides of the Atlantic.

CHAPTER THREE

DOLLARS AND POUNDS

With the end of the Cold War and the diminished emphasis on the Anglo-American security relationship, economic ties between the United States and Great Britain have grown in importance. Just as defense strategies have changed in light of the collapse of communism, so too have economic realities been transformed by the ascendance of the European Union. Anglo-American trade has become more complicated due to the existence of the EU, but both countries could profit greatly from the rise of this latest incarnation of what began in 1951 as the European Coal and Steel Community.

Like other parts of the relationship, the economic linkage dates back to the years when the American colonies were dominated by superpower Britain. Between 1700 and 1780, British overseas trade doubled, and from 1783 onward—after the American Revolution—it continued to grow rapidly. Among other facets of the two countries' trade ties, the newly born United States became Britain's most important source of raw cotton and was an important market for finished British textiles.

In the nineteenth century, the "Bill on London" was a widely accepted short-term credit instrument, financing not only British trade but also many U.S. import and export businesses. London's securities markets bankrolled capital projects such as bridges and railroads around the world, including ventures in the United States.

Legislation passed in the 1840s officially committed Great Britain to free trade, and the nation's tariff-free "open ports" helped stimulate expanded international trade. The open-ports principle and the heritage of Richard Cobden and opposition to the protectionist Corn Laws remain significant today. Former Foreign Secretary Douglas Hurd says: "The importance of Britain is not that we're the leading economic power. We're not. The importance is that we're free trade."[1]

Chancellor of the Exchequer Kenneth Clarke underscored Hurd's point in describing the issues underlying Anglo-American economic cooperation:

> There is something about Anglo-Saxon capitalism that is markedly different from Japanese capitalism and continental European capitalism as well. . . . The British and the Americans believe in competitive free markets and deregulated and flexible economies. We are not dirigiste. We are not hostile to foreign investment. We are not state traders. We are not attracted by the corporate state.[2]

Along the same lines, Alistair Hunter, executive chairman of the British-American Chamber of Commerce, says that Great Britain is appealing to the United States because "Britain is an enterprise society rather than a regulatory one."[3] This economic relationship can be evaluated on several levels: the many statistics that reflect an enormous amount of activity, and the more theoretical elements of economic changes that will reshape the global marketplace and the dealings of all who participate in it.

ANGLO-AMERICAN TRADE AND INVESTMENT

Beyond philosophy, the statistical picture of Anglo-American trade depicts a solid relationship:

- British exports of goods to the United States in 1996 were worth £20 billion/$33 billion. This was an increase of 11 percent over 1995, but Great Britain's share of the U.S. import market in goods in 1995 was 3.6 percent, a decline from roughly 6 percent several years earlier. Great Britain ranks seventh among U.S. import sources, behind Canada, Japan, Mexico, Germany, China, and Taiwan. (Overall, Great Britain exports more than a quarter of what it produces, a larger share than that of the United States or Japan.)

- British imports of goods from the United States in 1996 were worth £23 billion/$38 billion, an increase over 1995 of 7 percent, compared to a 3 percent U.S. export increase to the rest of the EU. Great Britain is the fourth-largest export market of the United States (after Canada, Mexico, and Japan).

- British exports of services (ranging from computer programming to tourism) to the United States in 1995 were worth £11 billion/$19 billion. Great Britain ranked first in this field, providing 13.6 percent of U.S. imports of services. This is a good illustration of the growing importance of exporting services in addition to goods.

Investment, rather than trade, is becoming increasingly dominant in the economic give-and-take between the two nations. The United States is the largest outside investor in Great Britain, and Great Britain is the largest outside investor in the United States (surpassing Japan as of 1994).

In 1979, British investments in the United States amounted to $15 billion; by 1995 that figure had reached $132 billion, which is 24 percent of the total foreign direct investment in the United States. Some of America's best-known companies are British owned, including Burger King, Dunkin' Donuts, and Holiday Inn.

By 1996, U.S. investment in Great Britain exceeded $102 billion, which is 17 percent of total U.S. overseas investment. U.S. industry commits more investment to Great Britain than to Germany, France, and Italy combined. More than 4,500 U.S. companies are established in Great Britain. Such U.S. investment helps create upwards of 20,000 jobs for British workers each year.

Another dominant characteristic of the British economy is its strength as a provider of services such as banking, law, insurance, shipping, computer programming, market research, communications, and other business essentials. For about 200 years (excluding times of war), Britain's trade in services has been in surplus. In 1994, services accounted for 72 percent of Great Britain's gross domestic product (GDP): £417 billion/$692 billion. More than 16 million British workers were employed in the services field, 76 percent of the work force.[4]

This is a giant industry in itself. For example, in London alone, financial, professional, and business-service companies employ 850,000 people. London ranks first in foreign-exchange trading, with 27 percent of the global market share; and first in international trade in equities, with a 60 percent share; and first in international bank lending, with a 17 percent share. In the legal profession, fourteen of Europe's fifteen biggest law firms are headquartered in London.[5] More than 500 banks from 70 countries have offices in London, compared with 280 in Paris and 250 in Frankfurt.[6] This list can be extended almost indefinitely, but beyond specific examples is the important general point that Great Britain is positioned to be a principal provider of the services that make the world economy work.

The facts about rates of investment flowing in both directions across the Atlantic are important, as is the emphasis on services that Great Britain offers. But what make these matters especially significant are the joint efforts by these two countries to enhance cooperation—to use investment to pull the nations closer together and to use services to establish improved trilateral linkage among the United States, Great Britain, and the EU.

The 17 percent ($102 billion) of U.S. overseas investment that Great Britain receives is 41 percent of total U.S. investment in the EU. Financial services (other than banking) and manufacturing account for 42 percent and 27 percent, respectively, of U.S. direct investment in Great Britain.

The Invest in Britain Bureau, part of the Department of Trade and Industry (DTI), aggressively seeks inward investment from throughout the world. In the United States, it has principal offices in New York, Atlanta, Chicago, and Los Angeles. Its pitch is straightforward: "We can provide practical help and advice on all aspects of setting up in the U.K., including site-finding, visit programs, information on local, regional, and national incentives, details of work permits and immigration law, worker availability and skills, subcontractors and suppliers, and information on European markets, E.U. rules, and other aspects of the operating environment."

In 1995–96, of 477 successful inward investment projects, 208 (44 percent) came from the United States. (Germany was in second place with 58 projects.) The year's projects created more than 48,000 new jobs; the American ventures produced almost 21,000 of these.[7] Among the U.S. investments during the year were these: Ford spent £330 million/$548 million to expand its plant in Wales; Digital Equipment expanded its operations in Scotland, doubling its work force to 600 after one year of production; Pfizer expanded its operation in England with an investment of £50 million/$83 million; and Hewlett-Packard opened a new £5-million/$9-million research and development facility in Ipswich and announced plans for a £19-million/$31-million laboratory in Bristol.

The trend continues. In 1997, Microsoft Corporation announced that it would spend £48 million/$80 million to establish a research laboratory in Cambridge, in collaboration with Cambridge University. This is the computer company's first overseas research facility. Microsoft will also invest £10 million/$16 million in a fund to support technology start-up ventures in the Cambridge area. Behind this move is the recognition that British brainpower can be a valuable asset for Microsoft, and the best way to tap into that asset is to foster research and product development in Great Britain.[8]

Andrew Fraser, director of the Invest in Britain Bureau, says that inward investment has been spurred by Great Britain's trend of deregulation and privatization. American companies have taken advantage of the opportunity to invest in newly privatized British utilities companies; for example, the U.S. company Cinergy acquired Midlands Electricity. Fraser also says that Britain is not resisting this globalization of its economic base; there is little detectable economic xenophobia about foreign investment. Britain is so focused on job creation, says Fraser, that there is minimal worry about the flood of investors from overseas.[9] Addressing the same issue, Chancellor Kenneth Clarke noted in 1995 that inward investment in Britain since 1979 had created or safeguarded more than 600,000 jobs.[10]

Along these lines, officials working on Great Britain's investment effort make objective judgments about whether the outside investor or Britain itself will reap the most long-term benefits. One DTI official notes: "We don't want to make U.S. companies more competitive against U.K. companies. We're looking at what's good for Britain. But we will help a company such as Motorola export from the U.K. to Germany because it employs people, manufactures, and pays taxes here."

As for selling points in their courtship of U.S. investors, British officials cite a "comfort level" based on the language, culture, legal system, and familiarity with the country derived from tourism. Great Britain seems less "foreign" to Americans than almost any other country, and that contributes to a sense of security for corporate executives deciding where to invest their capital.

While U.S. investment is being recruited, efforts are under way by another DTI program, North America Now, to get more British exports into the United States (and into Canada and Mexico). This is a sophisticated venture, with a USA Helpdesk in London that provides British businesses with advice about working in U.S. markets. In addition to a range of literature, the project features business executives on loan to the

DTI who provide free consultations about exporting. Also available is a service that facilitates getting needed manufacturing licenses and establishing joint ventures, joint marketing agreements, and transfer-of-technology arrangements. This broad array of offerings is designed partly to entice more small and medium-sized British businesses into exporting in order to build an expanded long-term export base. In the United States, as part of this program, British consulates provide further support: lists of lawyers, accountants, bankers, and other professionals; market assessments; reports about trade fairs; publicity; and general advice from the diplomatic corps's commercial officers.

The U.S. government cooperates with similar assistance based in its London embassy. There the U.S. Commercial Service staffs the American Business Information Center, which in 1996 responded to 15,500 phone inquiries and 2,100 letters or faxes from British firms looking for U.S. business contacts. During the year, the Commercial Service also produced eighty-three market research studies covering all the British industries with the best export potential for U.S. firms.

Although investment ventures vary greatly in size, some of the largest have significant economic impact. British Airways (BA), for example, is in the midst of a six-year (1996–2002) $17-billion program of investments in the United States. The bulk of this is a $10.8-billion purchase of Boeing airplanes. This means that in Washington State, the communities close to Boeing will receive an average of about $4.6 million a day in BA spending during the six years. Similarly, Cincinnati will see $11 million a month in BA expenditures for the General Electric engines that will power the Boeing planes. BA will also spend $5.9 billion on staff, marketing, fuel, and other U.S. operating costs. An additional $300 million will be spent on property, computer hardware, and other capital items.[11]

Another element of the transatlantic effort is what one British trade official calls "the devolution of economic responsibility in the U.S." U.S. governors and mayors are regularly visiting Britain (among other countries) to promote their exports and to tout their states and cities as attractive sites for investment. Texas is an example of a state with strong trade links to Britain. Britain is the second-largest foreign investor in Texas, trailing only Japan. As of mid-1997, there were 310 British companies operating in Texas (second to Canada). Great Britain sends £1.3 billion/$2.1 billion in exports to Texas and receives roughly the same amount in imports from the state.

THE GATEWAY TO EUROPE

As intensive and successful as this Anglo-American activity has been, trade strategies are changing, principally to adjust to the realities of the European Union. Great Britain, rather than being just a target market in itself, is now also being viewed as a gateway to the larger EU market. This does not mean that Britain is being bypassed by investors and traders. Rather, it signals a new opportunity for Britain, and particularly for its service industries, to cash in on growing U.S. interest in the EU.

The Commercial Service of the U.S. Department of Commerce has established Showcase Europe, which is designed to help U.S. companies develop a more regional perspective, rather than a country-specific one, in looking at Europe. The department's trade-promotion and business services are being repackaged to target regions within Europe as well as individual countries.

Charles Ford at the U.S. embassy in London says that Showcase Europe is basically "a government initiative responding to what the market has already done."[12] This is an important point. Government programs sometimes amount to nothing more than self-perpetuating projects that feature more flash than substance, and that are divorced from the realities of the marketplace. That is not the case in this instance; the market forces are real, and the government's effort has proved genuinely helpful.

The regional emphasis of Showcase Europe is rooted partly in the realization that U.S. business has not taken full advantage of the collective European market and some of its components. Jeffrey Garten, former under secretary of commerce and now dean of the Yale School of Management, said in 1994 that the Commerce Department's objective "is to try to raise company marketing efforts in other key European countries up to the existing level in the U.K. Germany, Italy, France, and Spain offer the largest potential. The potential is enormous. If we could attain the same share of the rest of the European Union as U.S. exports now have in Britain, U.S. exports to Europe would increase by as much as $50 billion—almost 50 percent more than today.[13]

Commerce Department officials note that U.S. businesses based in Great Britain are increasingly looking at more than just Great Britain. For instance, Fruit of the Loom operates in Londonderry, Northern Ireland, not only producing its products for the British market but also coordinating all of its European business from there. Andrew Fraser of the Invest in Britain Bureau reports that 68 percent of U.S. management functions for Europe are now based in Great Britain.[14]

The British government has been quick to enhance the country's role as Europe's entry point. A project called Gateway to Europe was created to assist companies wanting to expand into Europe and seeking advice about market conditions, logistics, standards, packaging, advertising, public relations, design, and other services. Of particular interest to the DTI staff members working on this project are U.S. companies that do business in Great Britain but have not yet reached the point of investing in a plant or jobs in Britain. If they are cultivated now, they might eventually decide to do so. Gateway prospects are asked to call a DTI official in either New York or London and are promised that within a week of their inquiry they will receive a list of service providers with pan-European experience. (The British service businesses are not given the U.S. company's name, so they cannot solicit directly.) Along similar lines, British trade officials working in the United States talk about the "Interstate to Europe," urging American companies to take advantage of the familiar language and culture in Britain en route to the mysterious continent across the Channel.

Nothing in all this activity is revolutionary in the sense of remaking the science of business recruitment. The key to the importance of these ventures is their pervasiveness and intensity. Also, both U.S. and British officials apparently recognize that the relationships most likely to enhance trade over the long term are those that are business-to-business rather than government-to-government. To that end, government should move as promptly as possible from being instigator to being facilitator.

An example of this process at work is the Transatlantic Business Dialogue. Meeting first in Seville, Spain, in November 1995 and then in Chicago a year later, this gathering of business leaders, organized initially by U.S. Commerce Secretary Ron Brown, helps define what needs to be done to improve transatlantic trade. Special emphasis is placed on lowering governmental barriers. For example, the Information Technology Agreement to eliminate tariffs on information technology (IT) products percolated up from the Seville conference. Foreign Secretary Malcolm Rifkind noted that this field employs more than 1.25 million people in the United States, and that Scotland produces 10 percent of the world's personal computers. Therefore, he said, "opening up IT markets—moving toward zero-to-zero tariffs, mutual recognition of product testing and certification—is enormously relevant to economic success and jobs on both sides of the Atlantic."[15]

Similarly, businesses critiqued the U.S. Food and Drug Administration (FDA) for requiring totally separate testing processes despite U.S. and some European standards being so similar. In response, the FDA relaxed its position, reducing the time required for making new drugs available. Foreign Secretary Rifkind also took note of this progress, citing the FDA's granting easier access to U.S. markets for Glaxo Wellcome, the British-based pharmaceutical giant. Within six weeks of the FDA's announcement, said Rifkind, the company's stock value rose £600 million/$996 million "as the markets recognized the prospect of more sales and profits, and that means more jobs."[16]

JOINT VENTURES

The growing closeness between U.S. and British business is illustrated on a grand scale by the proposed alliance between American Airlines (AA) and British Airways (BA). The plan has three main elements:

- Coordination of all passenger and cargo services the two airlines operate between the United States and Europe.
- Codesharing, which involves American Airlines putting its "AA" designator code on the transatlantic services of British Airways and its flights beyond its European gateways, while British Airways puts its "BA" code on American's comparable service across the Atlantic and beyond U.S. gateways. For passengers, this simplifies ticketing, as if only a single airline was involved.
- Creation of a fully reciprocal frequent flyer program.

This would not be a merger, but rather a cooperative relationship that is unusual in the sense that it would establish a common pool for revenues produced on the shared AA-BA routes.

For the passenger, the system would make easier what has sometimes been unpleasantly complex travel. Someone wanting to travel from Tucson to Berlin, for example, could call a travel agent who would find a Tucson-Chicago-London-Berlin itinerary listed as a single airline route. It would actually be a combination of AA and BA service, but the passenger could buy a single ticket, use a single baggage-handling system, and find coordinated arrival and departure times for the connections on all three legs of the trip. Regardless of which carrier's aircraft this passenger was on at various stages of the trip, the entire ticket price would go into the revenue pool.

This alliance will happen only if the U.S. and British governments agree to an open-skies policy that would replace the current Bermuda 2 Agreement, which was enacted in 1977 and has restricted air service between the United States and Great Britain. This will be a political as much as an economic decision. Under the current rules, British airlines have benefited from controlled competition, but such limitations have become archaic, particularly in light of other bilateral open-skies agreements and the EU's own open-skies policy that went into effect in 1997.

An Anglo-American open-skies agreement would, among other features, allow more airlines to have competitive access to London's Heathrow Airport, which is Europe's busiest. Not only American Airlines but also other carriers would be able to purchase new gate slots, which has been hard to do under the Bermuda 2 rules. This fact undercuts the argument that the alliance would be anticompetitive, allowing the AA-BA team to dominate the market unfairly. Under open skies, the current combined American Airlines and British Airways 61 percent share of the U.S.-London market would be expected to decline to 41 percent as other carriers take advantage of this new access to Heathrow.

Substantial economic impact would be produced by the alliance and other business generated by the open-skies agreement. By the fifth year of the relationship, an additional $28.5 billion in annual economic activity is expected in the United States: $9.1 billion in expenditures by foreign visitors; $3.7 billion in expenditures by American and foreign airlines; $4.2 billion in new aircraft purchases from U.S. manufacturers; $7.9 billion in additional imports of manufactured goods (plus an unquantified increase in service exports); and $3.6 billion in annual foreign investment.[17] According to British Airways, similar but less specific projections indicate that Great Britain would also reap considerable benefit from the plan. During this same five-year period, the number of weekly flights between the United States and Great Britain would almost double. The ripple effects of such an increase in traffic are hard to project, but almost certainly the added ease of transatlantic travel would enhance and expand Anglo-American business relationships.

Another combination of giants is the purchase by Merrill Lynch and Company, the largest American brokerage firm, of Mercury Asset Management Group PLC for £3.5 billion/$5.3 billion. Mercury is Britain's top-ranked money manager, with £112 billion/$170 billion in assets.[18] The deal, announced in November 1997, illustrates U.S. financial institutions' recognition of the importance of establishing themselves more firmly in Europe.

This flood of projects and the statistics they generate can be overwhelming, swamping those who want to see a more precisely drawn picture of the Anglo-American economic relationship. Such precision may be hard to come by because so much is going on, but the sheer volume itself means something. Only in a fundamentally healthy relationship will this level of activity occur.

TOURISM

A more traditional but still enormously important element of the Anglo-American economic relationship is tourism. Great Britain is the second-largest (after Japan) source of tourists visiting the United States. In 1995, more than 3 million British visitors spent £5 billion/$8 billion in the United States. The top destinations were New York City, Miami, Orlando, Los Angeles, and San Francisco.[19]

Also in 1995, more than 3 million Americans traveled to Great Britain. That was the largest contingent from any single country and was 14 percent of the total of Great Britain's foreign visitors. The Americans spent about £2 billion/$3.3 billion, which is 17 percent of the total spent by overseas visitors. As spenders, Americans lead the rest of the pack by a large margin; Germans are second, with an 8 percent share. The Americans' spending is roughly 5 percent of the £38 billion/$63 billion that tourism, including that by British residents, generates for the British economy. The British Tourist Authority estimates that 1.7 million British jobs are supported directly or indirectly by tourists' spending.[20]

British and U.S. tourism officials expect steady increases in the number of visitors and the amount of money they leave behind. The indirect benefits also are substantial; the familiarity with a country that a tourist may develop can lead to that same person eventually doing business there.

THE EU'S IMPACT ON U.S.-BRITISH ECONOMIC RELATIONS

As with security issues, the economic relationship between the United States and Great Britain should not be viewed in isolation. The European Union's impact on the U.S.-British partnership is large and growing.

Predictions differ about whether that impact is likely to be positive or negative. James Schlesinger, former U.S. secretary of defense, secretary of energy, and CIA director, has voiced a pessimistic view:

> Almost unavoidably the single market will be a vehicle for joint discrimination against the United States. One may accept European assurances that there is no desire or intention to create a high-barrier

Fortress Europe. That barriers may be no higher in absolute terms does not mean they will be no higher in relative terms. After all, the purpose of the single market is to eliminate internal barriers, which inherently means increased joint discrimination against the outside world. Moreover, the process of negotiation and accommodation will normally be at the expense of those who do not have to be accommodated in that process.[21]

On the other hand, the optimistic outlook has its supporters, such as Great Britain's Malcolm Rifkind: "The Single Market has opened new opportunities not only for its members but also for the rest of the world. Imports to the E.U. have risen, not fallen, since its creation. Regional and global liberalization are two sides of one coin."[22] Tony Blair has been a bit more cautious, noting the complexity of the issue: "We need a framework within which we can deal with the economic disputes that are certain to arise between the two sides of the Atlantic. The E.U. is a frustrating partner for the U.S. There is no one center of power. . . . The relationship will in reality need to pass through London, Paris, and Bonn as well as Brussels. Cooperation and consultation on this axis needs to be reinforced."[23]

The legalistic view would seem to be on the side of the optimists. Rules enforced by the World Trade Organization (WTO) guarantee that neither the EU nor the United States can turn itself into a tariff-protected fortress. This issue is important because the stakes are huge: the EU and the United States together account for about half of world trade, the EU 37 percent and the United States 14 percent. As British scholar Stephen Woolcock has noted, the central question is "whether the two leading heavyweights of the international trading system will cooperate as trading partners or seek to score political points off each other in a way that may ultimately undermine business confidence in continued stable economic links."[24]

The unofficial attitude within the British Foreign and Commonwealth Office also seems relatively sanguine. One official notes that the EU's planned expansion works against the notion of a fortress because "the walls would have to keep expanding"—probably more trouble than it would be worth. Also cited is the lack of purpose for protectionism: "Why do people construct fortresses? Because they're afraid. The EU—so big, so economically powerful—has no reason to be fearful."

A principal reason that the "fortress" approach will not take hold is that such a strategy has been made obsolete by the technologies so important to international trade. Malcolm Rifkind has said about this: "Modern technology and capital investment cross national boundaries ever more easily. The market finds a way around the barriers erected by politicians. Trying to shield industry from the need to compete and in-novate to attract customers, offers no reliable long-term protection for industry or for workers."[25]

The nature of global economics today works against protectionism. RAND vice president David Gompert offers a good summary of this case:

> The European economy cannot thrive indefinitely on intra–E.U. trade. Its most dynamic industries—information technology and pharmaceuticals, for example—cannot be world class if shielded from North America and East Asia. Europe needs access to those markets and to their software, chips, labs, and competitive pressure. Europe's participation in the integrated world economy—the prem-ise, after all, of the creation of the single European market—should grow and become politically irreversible. Except for agriculture and a handful of other noncompetitive sectors, globalist interests, in-cluding Europe's own multinational enterprises, appear to have got-ten the upper hand over protectionist interests.[26]

Douglas Hurd points out, nevertheless, that "there's a bit of protec-tionist in us all."[27] A case in point is the banana battle that has been brewing recently. In 1993, the EU (then the European Community [EC]) adopted a system that guarantees to banana producers in current or former British and French colonies a share of the EU market, which, for whatever reason, has the world's highest per capita consumption of bananas. At the same time, the EU imposed a quota on Central and South American bananas, where U.S. companies such as Chiquita and Dole dominate the business. The Clinton administration, proclaiming itself the champion of free trade, complained to the WTO, which ruled that the EU quotas unfairly restricted the U.S. companies' access to the European market.[28]

This is the kind of minibattle that will be waged as the remaining overtly protectionist barriers are chipped away. In the grand scheme of things, such contests are unlikely to cause much damage, although some U.S. military officials fear that in the banana case the WTO decision may prompt current Caribbean banana farmers to switch to the drug trade. The EU is providing £96 million/$160 million in grants to help Caribbean growers switch to other, presumably legal, ways to earn their living.

On the larger scale of U.S.-EU trade, matters are moving ahead relatively smoothly. So far, although trade between the United States and Europe as a whole is more than $200 billion a year, U.S. involvement with the EU has had a definite British slant. More than 40 percent of U.S. investment in the EU is in Great Britain. This apparent pro-British tilt by the Americans has, however, provided fuel for anti-EU sentiment in some quarters in Great Britain. Atlanticism is seen as a safe haven by Euroskeptics who theorize that the United States is a more reliable and less intrusive partner than the increasingly powerful EU. In other words, "Who needs the EU when we have America?" Asian countries, while not British trade partners at the level of the United States, are also seen as alternatives to Europe.

Tony Blair addressed this issue before the 1997 election: "The Euroskeptics sometimes suggest that the high level of inward investment in the U.K. demonstrates that we could go it alone. But they miss the point. The Japanese, the Americans, and the Koreans invest here because we are part of the European Union. If they see us slipping to a second tier, they will put their investment elsewhere."[29] Alistair Hunter of the British-American Chamber of Commerce makes the same point. He reports that "the more thoughtful U.S. businessmen say, 'At some point you have to become more involved in the E.U. or we'll have to transplant our investments to the continent.' "[30] So far this kind of pressure has been relatively gentle, but it is one of the factors in the discussion about Europe that became a crucial element in Britain's 1997 elections and will continue to be debated during the next several years.

There is no denying the growing importance not only of the EU as an international economic power but also of the European states, collectively and individually, as British trading partners. By the early 1990s, Western Europe took nearly two-thirds of Britain's exports, while trade with Commonwealth countries declined in importance. During the 1980s, the United States was Great Britain's largest single market, but it was overtaken in 1990 by Germany. Germany is also Britain's largest single supplier. In 1992, it took almost 14 percent of Britain's exports and supplied 15 percent of its imports.[31]

This shift in the relative importance to Great Britain of the United States and Europe requires readjustment of worldview. British journalist Henry Brandon wrote of this in 1992: "The fact that the British have now decided they must be part of the new Europe indicates the growing gravitational pull of the Community. The British know they will have to swallow hard to overcome their island psychology and their deep-seated attachment to century-old symbols of sovereignty as well as to face the devaluation of their 'special relationship' with the United States."[32]

British political leaders insist, however, that membership in the EU will not prove traumatic. The moderate view is that economic union does not require a substantive surrender of sovereignty, and that the transatlantic and transchannel relationships need not be mutually exclusive. Change is necessary, but absolutism is not, and therefore Anglo-American economic ties will not decline in importance.

EUROPEAN MONETARY UNION

Despite soothing prognostications from some, the sovereignty issue has loomed large in one of the most contentious EU-related debates, that about participation in the European Monetary Union (EMU). This issue created serious divisions in Britain's Conservative party during the 1997 campaign. John Major tried to make reluctance about joining the EMU a matter of patriotism and a wedge issue against Tony Blair and the Labour party. Instead, his advocacy of a wait-and-see approach to monetary union was attacked by the Tory right as weak-kneed and by party moderates (principally Chancellor Kenneth Clarke) as unrealistic.

The EU-related campaign squabbling reflects the public uneasiness that accompanies the EU's growing power. The British are not alone in their skepticism. A June 1997 survey conducted for the European Commission found that Finland, Sweden, and Denmark, as well as Great Britain, had substantial majorities opposed to a single currency. Even in Germany, a majority, although a smaller one, was in opposition. The British, with a 40 percentage-point margin of "against" over "for," were the second most negative, slightly behind the Danes.[33]

Despite uneven public support for the EU, Jacques Santer, president of the European Commission, forcefully argued that monetary union would produce valuable benefits: "lower transaction costs, lower interest rates, macroeconomic stability, trade facilitation, and less currency uncertainty helping cross-border trade and investment."[34] Nevertheless, many in Britain remained unconvinced. Journalist Martin Kettle of the Guardian summed up the unease permeating the British consideration of joining the EMU:

The single currency argument is inseparable from a passionately felt argument about British history and identity, in which the sense of

British independence is powerfully and offensively challenged by any attempt to assert that Britain's interests lie in a union with other European nations, especially Germany. Others believe . . . that these deep instincts are nothing less than a historic illusion. They believe that this vision of a free-standing Britain has been irrevocably shattered by the collapse of the British empire, by the unavailing struggle to claim superpower status in a world manifestly dominated by the United States, by the rise of the Asian-Pacific powers and not least, by the destruction of the British industrial base.[35]

On a less theoretical plane, British wariness about the EMU is grounded in fears that Great Britain's economy would be at a disadvantage in the new arrangement. For instance, personal borrowing in Britain, such as for mortgages, is mostly at variable interest rates, while fixed rates are most common in other EU countries. The British, therefore, would be particularly vulnerable to rate changes and other shifts in monetary policy enacted by a European central bank.

As the British grapple with their history and their future, the planned 1999 launch of the EMU draws closer. As of mid-1998, the theory most popular among British politicians, and probably among their constituents, was to adopt a wait-and-see position, forgoing membership in the EMU as it begins but keeping the door open to joining later. Whether other EU nations would allow a late entry remained open to question.

If the Blair government were forced to choose between only yes or no, it would face a daunting political challenge. A "yes" to EMU would mean (among other things) replacing the pound sterling with the new euro currency in 2002 and agreeing to adhere to EU monetary policy. Saying "no," assuming a delayed entry would not be allowed, would risk taking Britain out of Europe's (and thus the world's) economic mainstream. This would undermine the "gateway to Europe" pitch, and Britain might become a less desirable site for investment.

The Blair government in October 1997 decided to say neither "yes" nor "no," but rather to defer final judgment. In a statement to the House of Commons, Chancellor of the Exchequer Gordon Brown said: "We believe that, in principle, British membership of a successful single currency would be beneficial to Britain and to Europe. The key factor is whether the economic benefits of joining for business and industry are clear and unambiguous. If they are, there is no constitutional bar to British membership of EMU." But, he added, "applying the economic tests, it is not in this country's interest to join in the first wave of EMU," which starts at the beginning of 1999.[36]

There is much speculation about what the British timetable will be. The EMU currency, the euro, is scheduled to replace national currencies on January 1, 2002. If Britain holds a national election in 2001, a year before one must be called, EMU might be the dominant issue, and voters will be able to voice their opinion. Beyond the parliamentary election, the Blair government has pledged to submit any decision about joining EMU to a three-part test: a referendum; a vote in Parliament; and a cabinet decision. Only after all that would the government approach the EMU and express interest in joining.

The United States will probably have little patience for British dithering. The international economy certainly would benefit from EU countries meeting the principal EMU membership criteria: budget deficits below 3 percent of gross domestic product; public debt-to-GDP ratios below 60 percent; low inflation; and stable exchange rates. Massachusetts Institute of Technology professor Rudi Dornbusch wrote that the United States cannot lose from the EMU: "If it helps Europe grow, that is good for international prosperity. If it disarms the Bundesbank, with its deflationist tendencies, that's even better. If it creates better financial markets in Europe, U.S. investment houses and banks will be big players."[37]

Americans who make such judgments about the "good discipline" of EMU do not have to deal with the political repercussions of conforming to that discipline. Tony Judt of New York University notes that "by defining a strong euro as the main objective of union, and pegging painful social reforms and welfare cutbacks to that goal, Europe's leaders have played into the hands of critics from the political fringes. All across Europe, 'Brussels' is now attacked by demagogues as the symbol of rules and requirements that create local unemployment, cuts in government service, and economic stagnation." Outsiders might argue that this political discontent is insignificant when compared to global market forces. But as the 1997 French elections proved, "global market forces" don't vote.[38]

The single-currency debate illustrates how the United States is both a part of and separate from the life of Europe. Most Americans have only a vague idea of what the European Union is and know even less about EMU. The United States is, to some extent, above the battle. It can continue to play an important role in Europe's economy without worrying about a politically explosive issue such as seeing the dollar replaced by the euro. The continuing globalization of the economy may someday confront the United States with such decisions, but for now the United

States may simply watch while Great Britain and the other EU nations make their difficult choices.

The status of the dollar as principal international reserve currency could be affected by the euro in several ways. Leonhard Gleske, a former member of the Directorate of the Deutsche Bundesbank, observed that the international financial markets will gradually decide how much confidence they have in the European Central Bank and the euro as a reserve currency. In the meantime, with the popular deutsche mark superseded by the euro, the international position of the dollar may become stronger.[39] Fred Bergsten, director of the Institute for International Economics, writes: "The dollar will probably remain the leading currency indefinitely. But the creation of the euro will narrow, and perhaps eventually close, the present monetary gap between the United States and Europe. The dollar and the euro are each likely to wind up with about 40 percent of world finance, with about 20 percent remaining for the yen, the Swiss franc, and minor currencies."[40]

As Great Britain becomes ever more closely tied to its EU partners, fears occasionally surface about Anglo-American relations suffering as a result. Among many British political leaders, however, that notion is greeted skeptically. According to Chancellor Kenneth Clarke, "Britain's standing with the U.S. is enhanced, not weakened, by our standing in Europe. The U.S. judges us in part by the weight we carry in Bonn and Paris. Strong ties with Europe complement our strong ties with the United States."[41] Similarly, Tony Blair said in 1995: "Our road to maximum influence leads through Europe. If we are to be listened to seriously in Washington or Tokyo . . . we will often be acting with the rest of Europe. If we want to influence trade negotiations, we have to act as part of the E.U., the world's largest trading bloc. If we want to attract inward investment, it must be clear we are part of Europe."[42]

Although Great Britain plays a valuable gateway role in trade relations for U.S. businesses wanting to operate on the Continent, the political role is different. Britain is not a gatekeeper in terms of U.S. access to EU policy making. Nicholas Henderson, who served at various times as British ambassador to France, Germany, and the United States, said in 1997 that some in Britain "arrogantly think we should have that gatekeeper role, but the U.S. doesn't need it."[43]

In most situations, U.S. officials neither need nor want an interlocutor. Great Britain, in order to protect its own standing, has to keep a certain distance from the United States because its fellow EU members would not appreciate Britain acting as a U.S. stalking horse. How far that distance should be—the difference between "close" and "too close"—is difficult to determine.

As this multilateral relationship evolves, the U.S. position has been to nudge Great Britain toward becoming even more tightly tied to the rest of Europe. Political sensitivities about this can be easily inflamed. For instance, some in Great Britain note unhappily that U.S. officials use "integration" and "cooperation" interchangeably when discussing the British place in Europe. In Britain, some see a clear distinction between these two words. Many who are willing to cooperate react negatively to the idea of being integrated within Europe. That smacks of Eurofederalism and diminution of sovereignty. Although this may seem a minor semantic question, it is the kind of issue that can warm tempers during discussions about British-EU relations.

Douglas Hurd points out that Americans need to understand the cohesiveness of the EU. "There is not a triangle" of the United States, Great Britain, and the EU, he says, because "Europe negotiates as one."[44] That is a fundamental point that will require increasingly sophisticated U.S. diplomacy as the United States adjusts to the realities of the new Europe and as the EU becomes more assertive.

THE FUTURE OF TRANSATLANTIC TRADE

Despite the delicacy of intergovernmental maneuvering between the United States and Great Britain, at a business-to-business level, closeness between the two countries tends to be accepted without hesitation. Each has "most-favored-trading-partner" status in the eyes of the other. Alistair Hunter of the British-American Chamber of Commerce cites survey findings that "90 percent of British businessmen feel more comfortable doing business in the U.S. than in Germany." The reasons most often given, he says, are language, style of doing business, and temperament.[45]

Such closeness bodes well for the future, but plenty of questions arise about the evolving structure of the transatlantic relationship. Some support exists for a Transatlantic Free Trade Agreement (TAFTA). Among its backers have been Great Britain's Sir Leon Brittan (as vice president and chief trade negotiator of the European Commission), German foreign minister Klaus Kinkel, and Canadian minister for foreign trade Roy MacLaren.[46] Margaret Thatcher in 1992 endorsed the idea, saying, "In such a trading arrangement, Britain would have a vital role bridging that Atlantic divide—just as Germany should provide Europe with a bridge to the east and to the countries of the former Soviet Union."[47] Another supporter, Malcolm Rifkind, argued that "the removal of all transatlantic tariff and non-tariff barriers could mean at least $70 billion more trade."[48]

Support for TAFTA is not based solely on trade criteria. Charles Powell, top foreign policy aide to Prime Ministers Thatcher and Major, says, "I'd like to see it on political grounds as much as on economic grounds." He argues that TAFTA would be "another limb of the relationship" and adds that it "could be the missing dimension" in the Anglo-American partnership. "Without it," he notes, "there will be two competing systems": the United States and Europe.[49]

Some variations on TAFTA have also been suggested. While Ian Lang was president of Great Britain's Board of Trade, he said, " 'Transatlantic Open Markets' would be a good umbrella title for . . . E.U. and U.S. bilateral cooperation in areas such as mutual recognition of standards, competition policy, and the work of our Customs authorities." Lang also endorsed opening up government procurement and "new disciplines on subsidies."[50]

Douglas Hurd, while he was foreign secretary, did not call specifically for a TAFTA, but he did say that "Europe and the United States should commit themselves to tackle, and in due course dismantle, all the non-tariff barriers to transatlantic trade and to work together for free trade in services."[51] Similarly, Tony Blair, before becoming prime minister, said, "I urge E.U.-U.S. cooperation on the progressive elimination of all non-tariff barriers across the Atlantic to create a new Euro-Atlantic community."[52] When the New Transatlantic Agenda emerged from the 1995 Madrid summit, it contained no formal pledge about a TAFTA, but it did endorse a "new transatlantic marketplace" that would remove or reduce "barriers that hinder the flow of goods, services, and capital between us."[53]

These comments from such diverse sources may sound at first like a chorus of at least implicit support for a TAFTA, but there are some important differences among the respective viewpoints. The traditional function of free-trade treaties has been to eliminate or at least substantially limit tariffs. In transatlantic trade today, however, tariffs are not a major problem. The real barriers are incompatible product standards, procurement guidelines, subsidies, environmental regulations, tax rules, and other policies that act as de jure or de facto trade barriers. These are sensitive matters, often driven by domestic politics, and they are sometimes subtle in their application and effect. They do not lend themselves to elimination by a broad agreement, as tariffs do. That is why a veteran observer of transatlantic affairs, former U.S. ambassador to Britain Raymond Seitz, says, "TAFTA is an image in place of a policy."[54]

Non-tariff barriers can be hard to deal with because they are often not the product of governmental regulation but rather are imposed by the private sector. Standard setting by dominant companies can greatly influence market access, especially when compatibility with a design standard is important.[55] When these controls are coupled with statutory restrictions (often related to national security concerns), free trade suffers considerably.

In the global defense industry, the United States dominates and evidences little concern about the niceties of balanced trade. In 1995, the United States imported $500 million worth of European arms while exporting $3.1 billion to Europe. While the Americans may claim that the imbalance is due to their offering superior products, critics charge that they are engaging in blatant protectionism. One problem is the Pentagon's insistence that even when it buys foreign hardware, it usually must be built in the United States. For example, when General Dynamics agreed to buy engines for the Abrams tank from the German company Daimler-Benz Aerospace, it required that they be built under license in the United States.[56] The Germans do not like that practice, nor do the British. Great Britain is the world's second-largest arms exporter and does not want to face barriers, especially those erected by a friend.

In another area, Douglas Hurd has noted that "in the services sector, tariffs are not the issue; the problem is about being allowed to compete on equal terms with domestic suppliers."[57] Still another economic category, public procurement, which encompasses a $900-billion transatlantic market, also features obstacles that work against European companies.[58] The United States is a major contributor to such trade impairments because of the "Buy American" rules imposed at federal and state levels. Although the EU has no formal rules such as these, individual member nations do have policies supporting reliance on national suppliers to fulfill public contracts.[59]

"Buy American" provisions often are based on a pricing preference; for example, a 6 percent price preference for U.S. products in federal purchasing means that 6 percent is added to the quoted price of a supplier from another country before the bids are compared. In state and local purchasing, which accounts for about 70 percent of all government purchasing, "Buy American" provisions are common, especially in construction and mass-transit projects. Roughly two-thirds of the states have passed some form of "Buy American" legislation.[60]

The "Buy American" policies are seen by some in Europe as evidence of the residual protectionist culture of the United States. But while U.S. politicians may try to use "economic patriotism" to win votes, the public seems unmoved by appeals to buy American. A 1993 survey in the United States found that 73 percent of respondents said that they try to buy the best product, regardless of whether it is American made.[61]

All these issues should be addressed, but they do not readily lend themselves to the sweeping measures that presumably would make up a TAFTA. Governments that are determined to reduce these barriers can do so without a major treaty, and in some instances government involvement could be limited to providing the stimuli that will encourage businesses to shrink trade obstacles on their own. Another problem with TAFTA is cited by Beatrice Heuser: "A purely North Atlantic solution could not possibly be regarded as totally satisfactory. It would necessarily be seen as an extremely objectionable, indeed hostile, policy by the dynamic Far Eastern countries."[62]

The two biggest trading blocs, the EU and North American Free Trade Agreement (NAFTA) countries, are contemplating expansion. The desire to pull as many trade issues as possible within the governance of such treaty-based associations may nudge the transatlantic nations toward a TAFTA. But at least some, and perhaps most, of the trade benefits TAFTA would bring can be achieved without such a formal structure.

Solid ground exists on which to build a collegial future for Anglo-American economic relations. The likelihood of serious problems currently appears slight. Difficulties certainly would arise if the EU backslides on its free-trade promises, but doing so would be so obviously self-defeating that such a scenario is hard to envision.

Monetary union also promises to be one of the greatest shakes of the kaleidoscope, but unless it goes horribly wrong, the transatlantic business foundation should remain solid. Alistair Hunter says, "There is no common currency scenario that would chase away U.S. business."[63] The task for the United States and the European Union is to design a smooth transition into stable coexistence between dollar and euro.

On the U.S. side, the transatlantic trade relationship would be endangered if protectionism—one of those recessive genes in the American character—comes to the fore. Survey research conducted by the Times Mirror Center for the People and the Press during the early stages of the 1996 presidential race found that "the American public is two-minded about foreign trade, ideologically liberal by favoring free trade in principle but operationally conservative by emphasizing the need to protect U.S. products and particularly U.S. jobs from foreign competition. This two-mindedness notwithstanding, over the past year more events and shifts have occurred which play to the protectionist face of public opinion rather than to encouraging free trade." With a substantial percentage of workers worried about losing their jobs or taking salary cuts, and with even more concerned about their children's eventual ability to find decent jobs, free trade loses some of its appeal.[64]

The impact of this kind of opinion on public policy depends largely on the quality of leadership provided by elected officials and other opinion shapers. When a politician such as Pat Buchanan is loudly recruiting "peasants with pitchforks" and promising "to bring the new world order crashing down," protectionist sentiment may surge. But so far, the ascendance of such candidates and such opinions has been short-lived. Absent economic upheaval in the United States, Buchanan, Ross Perot, and other outside-the-mainstream candidates are likely to see their bases of support shrink rather than expand. In Great Britain, similarly, attempts by the Conservative party and fringe candidates to rouse anti-Europe feelings during the 1997 campaign proved unproductive.

Nevertheless, trade politics remains unpredictable. In late 1997, Congress refused to give "fast-track" negotiating authority to President Clinton. This setback was engineered by Clinton's fellow Democrats and the labor unions, perhaps foreshadowing a fight about trade during the 2000 presidential campaign, particularly during the Democratic primaries.

Beyond these political matters, a key influence on transatlantic economic issues will be the goings on in other parts of the world. British trade officials, for instance, know that decisions must be made about priorities: should they play to strength, nurturing ties to the Continent and North America, or should they concentrate on areas where they are weaker, such as East Asia?

For the United States, the dilemma may be even more pronounced. As a Pacific as well as an Atlantic nation, the United States faces the perpetual task of keeping its equilibrium as it tries to reap the greatest benefits from its trading partners across both oceans. Also, U.S. decisions must be made about trade within the Western Hemisphere. In May 1997, officials from thirty-four American republics (only Cuba was uninvited) met in Belo Horizonte, Brazil, to discuss building a Free Trade Area of the Americas (FTAA). The goal of an FTAA is to have a free-trade organization that runs from Alaska to Tierra del Fuego, incorporating such disparate economies as those of the United States and Haiti. By comparison, the EU seems nicely homogeneous.

The 1991 Asuncion Treaty establishing Mercosur (Argentina, Brazil, Paraguay, and Uruguay) created a customs union with a common external tariff and the goal of gradually reaching a zero tariff for trade among its members. This was an important step toward establishing a common market of the Americas. The Belo Horizonte conference kept this process moving.[65] U.S. policy makers will have to determine the extent of American leadership in this venture and how commitments to an FTAA might affect other U.S. international trade policies. At another hemispheric summit in April 1998, leaders of the participating nations pledged to work toward a goal of creating the free-trade zone by 2005. If established, the FTAA would include 750 million people, more than double the EU's population. The gross domestic product of its members would be more than $9 trillion (with the United States accounting for eighty-five percent of this).[66]

Even optimists will have to admit that nothing about economics is certain. The business world will change steadily and rapidly, altering the rules and frames of reference of international trade. Increased globalization will mean that defining a "U.S. company" or a "British corporation" will become more difficult and less useful. In the United States and Great Britain, as elsewhere, adapting to such transformation will test the imagination and flexibility of the governmental and private entities that drive the business of doing business. It will also test the viability of the Anglo-American economic partnership.

CHAPTER FOUR

BEYOND MASTERPIECE THEATRE

"In taste and learning they are woefully deficient" was Frances Trollope's appraisal of Americans, in whose midst she spent almost four often un-happy years. Her *Domestic Manners of the Americans*, which was published in 1832, won her acclaim at home in Great Britain as a savvy judge of the upstarts across the Atlantic. Trollope's book was laced with caustic judgments about her subject. She noted that the greatest difference be-tween the English and the Americans was "the want of refinement" on the part of the latter. Trollope was also unimpressed by the democratic lifestyle in which Americans took such pride: "All the freedom enjoyed in America beyond what is enjoyed in England, is enjoyed solely by the disorderly at the expense of the orderly."

These critical opinions were reciprocated. One American hotel owner told his British guest, "Our manners are very good manners, and we don't wish any changes from England." Overall, wrote Trollope, there was a "national feeling of, I believe, unconquerable dislike, which evidently lives at the bottom of every truly American heart against the English."

The book was a great commercial success, controversial on both sides of the Atlantic for its depiction not just of the American character but also the Americans' support of egalitarianism and professedly populist democracy. Trollope made valid points about American slavery and mistreatment of Indians, but reserved particularly sharp barbs for what she considered to be inappropriate respect for lines between social classes. She took offense, for example, at some uncouth neighbors' "extraordinary familiarity" toward her. While she was in Washington, she visited Congress, whose members she found "sitting in the most unseemly attitudes, a large majority with their hats on, and nearly all spitting to an excess that decency forbids me to describe."[1] Trollope's son, novelist Anthony Trollope, shared some of her opinions about Americans, referring in his *Autobiography* to "the infinite baseness of their public life."[2]

Judgments about Americans and their culture have softened considerably in most British quarters since the Trollopes' times. Nevertheless, disdain and wariness about Americans remain, and not just in Great Britain. American cultural historian Richard Pells writes that many Europeans have felt free "to scorn America, much as the Greeks had condescended to Rome."[3]

The United States is too powerful to be only loved and to escape such criticism. It has, however, fared better in its relations with Great Britain than it has with some of its other friends. The reason for this is quite likely rooted in the ease of communication.

THE LANGUAGE

Between Great Britain and the United States, virtually all relationships, be they cultural or political, have a special character because of the common language. Former U.S. ambassador to Britain Raymond Seitz has noted that "in language, the fact is we are not separated even by dialect, and this means in a range of affairs we are able to communicate with each other with a facility not available in the relations of other major powers— we can talk to each other in nuance."[4]

In addition to the closeness it creates, the shared language can also foster rivalry. Ralph Waldo Emerson wrote in 1878, "It is certain that more people speak English correctly in the United States than in Britain."[5] H. L. Mencken, in *The American Language*, made the case for the existence of a unique, non-British tongue. Oscar Wilde noted in *The Canterville Ghost* that "we really have everything in common with America nowadays except, of course, language."

Linguistic divisions do exist. In the United States, a refined British accent is thought to sound "upper class," which carries with it the risk of seeming pretentious. When an American speaks (or tries to speak) with such an accent, it may be regarded by his or her listeners as an affectation.

For their part, many Britons speak with an accent that Americans find nearly incomprehensible. Any American who has watched British television series will almost certainly have had trouble with the elisions and slang, just as most Britons probably find urban America's street jargon and intonation impenetrable.

More generally, the United States, robust and brash, is seen by some as a menacing cultural imperialist. British writer Francis Williams has warned of the threat to "Englishness" created by the British accepting more of U.S. culture "than it is possible for our society to assimilate and still remain true to its own virtues." If this continues, he wrote in 1962, "we may kill much that gives to English life its color and zest and character . . . what is specifically English in our civilization."[6]

Fears of U.S. cultural intrusiveness are grounded in recognition of the economic giant's pervasive commercial presence. Without doubt, the United States dominates modern cultural media, such as television, film, and recorded music, but the menace this creates may tend to be overestimated, just as the resilience and adaptability of other countries' cultures may be underrated. The potency of outside influence has its limits, particularly when the country being affected is one such as Great Britain, with its own culture so vibrant and deep-rooted. Mutual enrichment is more likely than is usurpation.

LITERARY TIES

British poet Stephen Spender wrote during the 1970s that "English writers are . . . drawn to the United States by its immediately contemporary energy, just as American writers were, a hundred years ago, drawn to Europe by its past."[7] David Parker, director of the Dickens House museum in London, also appreciates the interaction of British and U.S. cultures. He says of U.S. influence: "It's the bellwether culture. It's the culture that makes things happen and makes things change. It reflects buoyancy, optimism, success, wealth." Despite this, he adds, "American culture doesn't threaten British culture."[8]

Such national self-confidence makes sense. In literature, for example, the dominance of Great Britain is unassailable. Long before there was a United States, there were Chaucer, Shakespeare, Milton, and many more contributors to the English language's treasury of intellectual wealth. The idea that the body of American literature could in some way surpass that of Great Britain is ridiculous.

The two countries' literary traditions are more shared than competitive.

British writers such as Charles Dickens are part of the fabric of American intellectual life. David Parker theorizes that Dickens's popularity in the United States is based primarily on the appeal of one work, "A Christmas Carol." He explains it this way: "Because of the Constitutionally secular nature of the United States, there is a need to find a secular Christmas. 'A Christmas Carol' stands to one side of Christianity, presenting the humanistic side of Christmas. . . . How many [American] schools don't put on a performance of 'A Christmas Carol'?"

This theory is appealing, partly because it is so unprovable. Parker also offers a more conventional explanation of Dickens's popularity: "Dickens is central to any culture that has undergone the exhilaration and agony of an industrial revolution. . . . We produced our great writers of the industrial revolution before anyone else did. Until you come to Dreiser and Steinbeck, American writers did not address such topics. Americans had turned instead to the frontier" as a source of inspiration for fiction.[9]

Whatever the reason, Americans do seem enamored of Dickens. Various editions of his works can be found in virtually every bookstore and in countless school curricula. Parker reports that a 1995 survey at Dickens House found that 34 percent of the museum's visitors came from the United States and only 11 percent from Great Britain, with another 20 percent from Japan.

Despite Dickens's current popularity, he has not always been held in high esteem by Americans. When his book *American Notes* was published in 1842, its decidedly mixed review of American life was seen as an affront by some American critics, particularly those disposed to being suspicious of Britain. For example, James Gordon Bennett, editor of the *New York Herald*, called Dickens "the most trashy . . . the most contemptible" of British visitors, "the essence of balderdash, reduced to the last drop of silliness and inanity."[10]

Dickens later became more admiring of America, especially during his second U.S. tour in 1867, and Americans set aside much of their criticism of him. Nonetheless, this criticism illustrates the sensitivity and tension that periodically surface in the cultural relationship between the two countries. A wariness that is grounded partly in jealousy and partly in arrogance is a function of the similarities of British and U.S. artistic expression. Criticism from a French or German would not be taken in the same way because, so the thinking goes, they don't know any better; they are true foreigners. But between Britons and Americans is a closeness that carries with it implicit obligations of courtesy, even though this may not always foster intellectual frankness.

Of the classic authors, Dickens has recently been challenged in U.S. popularity by Jane Austen, whose novels have been made into several successful films and television series, released in close succession. The 1995 showing of *Pride and Prejudice* attracted the largest audience in the history of the Arts and Entertainment cable channel. *Clueless*, a much modernized version of *Emma*, was especially popular among young movie-goers, most of whom had no idea who Jane Austen was. *Sense and Sensibility* starred Emma Thompson and Hugh Grant, whose box-office appeal pulled people into theaters.

This "discovery" of Jane Austen by new audiences gives new heart to those who cherish literacy. Assessing the audience appeal of the Austen movies, Henry Grunwald, former editor in chief of Time, Incorporated, wrote that "watching each of the Austen productions, I was struck by the good manners and the correct English—language representing manners of the mind. The contrast with the vulgarity of most other films and much of daily life brought me a sense of relief, of being in an oasis." Grunwald also cited survey research that found that "people—including young people—deplore the lack of civility and the disappearance of respect. Those are among the things they seem to find in Jane Austen. They also find excitement and passion, courage and independence, and they may be surprised to see that these are not undermined but reinforced by manners."[11]

There is no parochialism involved in Americans' interest in Jane Austen. While Dickens wrote *American Notes* and set some chapters of *Martin Chuzzlewit* in the United States, in all of Austen's novels there is only one brief and ambiguous reference to America, an overheard remark in *Mansfield Park*.[12] The latest movie versions of Austen's work are probably the key factor behind the spurt of interest. The Jane Austen Society of North America, comprising some of the writer's most devoted admirers, has only about 3,300 members, but that number represents a 46 percent increase from 1995 to 1996.

Grunwald's theory about Americans' yearning for a more polite society can perhaps be extended beyond Austen to include an exaggerated stereotype of English manners and mores. It is only in a mythic England that all was genteel and serene; Jane Austen's fictive politesse existed within a fragile bubble in a rough Britain. Nevertheless, the myth persists and is eagerly embraced by those Americans who look across the Atlantic and believe that they see "refinement."

Part of the London tourism boom among Americans during the mid-1990s can be attributed to a nostalgia for what is considered "traditional" culture. One American resident in London observed: "The key to London right now has nothing to do with Tony Blair being Jack Kennedy. It has a lot more to do with Marlowe and Shakespeare. The thing is, the English do English."[13] The enthusiastic response to the opening of the new Globe Theatre in 1997 is one part of this.

For their part, the British have much different literature-fueled impressions of America. They might read Mark Twain, F. Scott Fitzgerald, John Steinbeck, J. D. Salinger, or Norman Mailer and derive a variety of impressions from the authors' versions of America. No American writer holds the same exalted place in British life that Shakespeare, Dickens, and a few others do in American culture. That is not to say that the American influence is not profound; it merely works principally through other, newer media.

COMMERCIAL CULTURE

Although the dominance of the U.S. manufacturing base has slipped in some fields, such as the automobile and consumer electronics industries, the United States remains unequalled as an exporter of things cultural. Through television, cinema, and recorded music (plus other manifestations, such as advertising and fast food), the United States shapes substantial parts of the life of the world.

The cultural balance between the United States and Great Britain sometimes gets knocked askew. For instance, in exchange for Jane Austen's Bennet sisters, the United States offers the "*Baywatch* babes." To defenders of British culture, this may seem ample proof that the barbarians—American cultural imperialists—are at the gate.

The *Baywatch* story line centers on the exploits of scantily clad female lifeguards. It is unlikely to be confused with *Masterpiece Theatre*. Of course, Americans merely export *Baywatch*; Britons watch it. At its peak, the show had ten million British viewers. One British cultural expert says only half-jokingly that in Great Britain *Baywatch* babe Pamela Anderson "is one of the best-known living Americans."

In late 1996, the audience fell to six million, and the British network ITV dropped the show. Six months later, series star and executive producer David Hasselhoff brought several of his "lifeguards" to London for a publicity tour and promised that the show would increase its "babe count." He said, "We have gone overboard on the babes this season." That was all ITV needed to hear. *Baywatch* was promptly returned to the network's schedule. (To be fair to Hasselhoff, it should be noted that he added, "We will still have family stories and plenty of action.")[14]

U.S. media products other than television programs also are ubiquitous in Great Britain. For example, 95 percent of cinema admissions in Britain are to American films.[15] The insidiousness of such dominance depends on the predisposition of those who observe it. To some, this is evidence of dangerous Americanization of British culture and underscores Britain's failure to compete effectively in the cultural marketplace. Others will shrug and ask what harm is being done.

Few of the evils depicted in the entertainment media are uniquely American, and those that are do not necessarily pose a threat to the British. Some Britons worry, for example, about U.S.-made television programs and movies that glorify America's gun culture, but Great Britain's comprehensive gun-control laws presumably neutralize effects of these messages.

Mere presence does not necessarily constitute usurpation. For instance, the growing (but still-marginal) popularity of American-style football in Great Britain does not undermine British football (soccer), cricket, or any other British sport. As is the case with free trade, a healthy marketplace can expand to accommodate competition.

That, at least, is the theory. In practice, British filmmaking and television production sometimes seem overwhelmed in terms of their ability to compete with American media products. British television efforts, such as the *Prime Suspect* series and *Monty Python's Flying Circus* and its descendants, receive acclaim from U.S. critics but usually end up on the Public Broadcasting System (PBS) or cable outlets and garner only a tiny share of the U.S. audience.

Anyone who scans a week's television fare will see that a fundamental imbalance exists. Viewers of British broadcast networks have the option of watching plenty of U.S. programs, while U.S. television watchers (except those wholeheartedly devoted to PBS) will rarely find a British product on the schedule. Cable channels in both Great Britain and the United States greatly expand the number of offerings, but the difference in the availability of U.S. and British programs on cable is much the same as on the broadcast channels.

The British movie industry, however, is making a comeback, both with its own product and with facilities that are used by others. The recent highpoint in British cinema in terms of commercial success was *Four Weddings and a Funeral*, which grossed about $250 million, making it the most successful British movie ever at the box office. In 1998, *The Full Monty* won an Academy Award nomination for "Best Picture."

Financial triumphs do not come often, but the movie industry can make money in other ways. For instance, the new Leavesden studio north of London won the contract for shooting the next *Star Wars* trilogy. The producers, Lucasfilm, will build their own high-tech studios as part of the Leavesden complex, bringing important new cinema technology to British moviemakers.

Leavesden has the largest indoor studio in Europe and also features a 100-acre backlot, the biggest in the world. Plans exist for a movie-industry business park near the Leavesden studios. In London, meanwhile, Warner Brothers has opened a new animation studio, employing seventy animators. Also, Disney will be animating its remake of *Fantasia* in London.[16]

If there is a mass-media field in which the British have the upper hand, it is pop music. With more than 200 million British album and compact-disc sales in 1997, Great Britain's music industry is healthier than its U.S. counterpart. This strength has also given a boost to tourism. In Liverpool, for example, Beatles-related tourism in 1995 was worth $96 million to the city, and in London, the Rock Circus wax museum (part of the Tussaud's Group) attracted more than 700,000 visitors. Promoters of the new National Centre for Popular Music in Sheffield hope that it will rival Cleveland's Rock and Roll Hall of Fame.[17]

Americans and Britons will certainly continue to share the products of their entertainment media. They have enough in common in terms of language and heritage to make such give-and-take comfortable and commercially appealing. Similarly, some resentment about American dominance will always exist, but probably not to the point at which Britain tries to invoke cultural protectionism, such as the French—without much success—have periodically endorsed.

The arts provide insights into national life. For instance, the icons of the moment—Elvis Presley, the Beatles, whoever—say something about the larger societal context from which they emerge. Fictive as well as real figures do this: spy-novel heroes, for example. The transition from Ian Fleming's James Bond to John Le Carré's George Smiley was a shift from the derring-do of an Empire man to the subdued craftiness of an anachronistically honorable Cold Warrior. Changes in Britain's heroes have reflected changes in the nation itself.

THE ACADEMIC RELATIONSHIP

In addition to their obvious manifestations in the arts, Anglo-American cultural links have systemic elements that may be less visible but no less significant in reinforcing ties between the two countries. Among these links are the American studies programs at British universities, which are enjoying a surge in popularity among students. In 1967, six British universities offered an undergraduate degree in American studies, and there was one graduate program. In 1995, these numbers had risen to thirty-eight undergraduate and thirteen graduate programs.[18] Richard Pells of the University of Texas notes that by the 1980s, British students could remain in Great Britain "and be trained by British Americanists who were now confident of their ability to write about the United States with the same skill and archival sophistication as their American counterparts, and who thought of themselves not as outcasts or rebels but as academic insiders."[19] The reason for the surge in British academic interest in the United States is apparently twofold: long-standing fascination with the United States, made more timely by recognition that as the only superpower of the moment, the United States merits intensive study.

The Institute of United States Studies at the University of London is one of the older ventures in this field, begun in 1965. It is solely a graduate program, offering courses such as "American Foreign Policy after the Cold War," "Migration and Ethnicity in the United States, 1820–1880," and "Twentieth-Century American Fiction." It also sponsors conferences on topics such as "The Legacy of Franklin D. Roosevelt" and "Race and Racism in America and Britain."

Gary McDowell, an American who directs this University of London program, says that although the field is traditionally split between history and literature, the hot area of the moment is cultural studies. Younger academics, he says, are particularly intrigued by this topic. McDowell, who taught at Harvard Law School before coming to London, notes wistfully that "there's more interest in Madonna than in Madison."[20]

Enthusiasm for this field is not universal. One American scholar says that in some British academic circles, studying the United States is viewed with disdain. There is, he says, "a large strain of anti-American sentiment—condescension joined with jealousy." But McDowell says that such anti-Americanism is shortsighted, and he urges that scholars in each country increase their study of the other. "The U.K.," he says, "doesn't just need the U.S. The U.S. needs the U.K., and that's what gets forgotten."[21]

LINKING CULTURE AND TRADE

While these British academic approaches to Anglo-American relations continue to develop, renewed efforts are being made to integrate cultural affairs and economic development. The British Council, which may be characterized as something like the United States Information Agency, but less political, organizes programs that maintain a highly visible British cultural presence in the United States and elsewhere. The council does not concentrate exclusively on the well-known classic British arts, but prefers to emphasize contemporary offerings as well. David Evans, the council's director in the United States, says: "We're looking very much forward. Austen and Dickens can look after themselves. We want to give exposure to what is going on creatively in the U.K. now." This means, for example, bringing African-Anglo artists to the United States to visit African-American colleges. Although the council works throughout the world, it has a special affinity for English-speaking peoples with whom a common heritage is shared in some way or another. Cultural ties with the United States are particularly strong, says Evans, partly because of "the huge amount of movement of people between the two countries and interconnections at all kinds of levels."[22]

These interconnections take shape in a series of festivals held in the United States that showcase British culture and business. For example, "Britain Meets the Bay," held in San Francisco in 1997, featured three months' worth of British arts offerings: films; photographs, paintings, and prints by contemporary British artists (including the Prince of Wales); an exhibition arranged by the Royal Institute of British Architects; music ranging from Gilbert and Sullivan to contemporary British compositions; performances by the Royal Shakespeare Company; and many more events. Education programs included the Oxford and Cambridge University debating teams; seminars about Bloomsbury, Churchill, the European Union, and other topics; and distribution to Bay Area schools of 1,000 study packs including videotapes, CD-ROMs, and printed material about British studies.

This substantial British cultural presence was matched by trade programming, including "UK/US Partners in Technology," a weeklong conference, exhibition, and "matchmaking" project involving more than 100 British high-tech companies and a large number of their U.S. counterparts. For the general public, there was coordinated retail promotion of British consumer goods, such as porcelain, jewelry, and food.

"Britain Meets the Bay" was not an isolated event. Similar efforts go on continually throughout the United States, building new links and strengthening existing ties between the two countries. Although the hoopla attending such ventures may cause some observers to dismiss them as mere public relations froth, there is more to them than that. They raise the British profile in the United States and remind Americans of the common ground between the two nations and their peoples. Culture opens the door to trade, tourism, and other relationships, underscoring the comfort level that naturally exists in Anglo-American partnerships, particularly when compared to dealings with other countries whose cultures are less familiar to Americans.

THE EVOLUTION OF NATIONAL IDENTITIES

The cozy cultural affinity between the United States and Great Britain has endured since the days of the American colonies. Thomas Jefferson wrote, "Our laws, language, religion, politics and manners are so deeply laid in English foundations that we shall never cease to consider their history as part of ours, and to study ours [with theirs] as its origin."[23]

Whatever the political vicissitudes of the moment, that linkage remained. Churchill's conception of the "special relationship" was founded not just on shared policy goals, but also on the shared interests of English-speaking peoples and, more particularly, of Anglo-oriented cultures.

But the Anglo base of American life is not as dominant as it once was. Similar change, although to a considerably lesser degree, is occurring in Great Britain. In the United States, Anglos are expected to constitute less than 50 percent of the population by 2015, and Hispanics will surpass African Americans as the largest minority group. In Great Britain, the 1980s saw immigration overtake emigration, with most of the newcomers coming from the Caribbean, Asia, and Africa. In the 1990s, migration into Great Britain has averaged about 243,000 per year.

Racial and cultural identities are evolving throughout the world, and traditional lines are blurring. Interests and loyalties likewise are shifting. American scholar Henry Louis Gates, Jr., has noted that the British identity is "a contested space." He writes that former Conservative party chairman Norman Tebbit complained a few years ago

that when Britain's cricket team played one of the West Indian teams "our blacks" tended to root for the wrong side. How could they be truly British if they weren't rooting for the British team? And it's perfectly true that most black Brits fail the so-called Tebbit

test; collective allegiances don't always align themselves altogether
neatly. In Britain, the challenge is to figure out a vocabulary for
addressing the intersections of racial and national identities.[24]

More recently, Lord Tebbit told a Conservative party conference that
"multiculturalism is a divisive force" inconsistent with British tradition.
Party leader William Hague rebuffed Tebbit by praising blacks' and
Asians' "positive contributions to British life."[25]

The challenge for Great Britain is not unlike the one facing Americans.
Although race issues in the United States are tied to distinct national
identities less often than they are in Britain (the younger country is the
older immigrant society), the racial Balkanization of the United States
continues. Despite soothing rhetoric from national leaders, the de facto
social and economic segregation of many U.S. communities is evidence
of the deep-rooted resilience of this problem. Similar delineation can be
seen in London (with at least half a dozen boroughs that have 30 percent
or more minority residents) and in cities such as Leicester and Birming-
ham. In London's schools, 112 languages are spoken; similar figures are
found in the school systems of the biggest cities in the United States.

In Great Britain, minorities are truly that; they collectively number
about 3.3 million people, about 6 percent of the total population, which
in 1996 was approximately 56.3 million. Indians constitute the largest
group: 877,000, which is 27 percent of the total ethnic minority population. About 1.6 million people living in Britain are from the Indian
subcontinent, 875,000 are black, and 287,000 are other Asian.[26]
Minority-group members are far less likely than whites to live in Britain's
affluent areas. In 1994–95, for example, 60 percent of Pakistani/Bangla-
deshi households lived in council estates and other low-income areas,
compared with 19 percent of white households.[27]

The United States and Great Britain are by no means the only countries coming to grips with diversity. As international mobility increases
and the significance of traditional political boundaries decreases, national
homogeneity will become less common and issues related to population
shifts will multiply. That is the state of the world, but in terms of the
state of U.S.-British relations, questions remain about whether the common cultural foundation will be able to support a structure that now
branches off in so many directions.

The arithmetic of population shifts indicates that Great Britain's
changes are far less pervasive, and thus far less influential, than are those
in the United States. Nevertheless, the definition of "Britishness" remains

a contentious issue. American scholar Kathleen Paul has noted that the diversity of the new Britain makes unrealistic the idea of defining "a singular fixed national identity for all British citizens." She says that the claim of Britishness is justified for all those who live there, and she urges adoption of "a new, flexible, and inclusive definition of Britishness" to accommodate the demographic makeup of the nation.[28]

STRIKING A CULTURAL BALANCE

However the British define themselves and however their population evolves, their cultural prospects will remain closely linked to those for Americans. Language is an important part of this. For instance, English is the dominant language of the Internet. (This particularly distresses some in France, who want, but probably won't get, a French-language Internet.)

Aside from language, U.S. economic power presumably will continue to drive commercial culture, at least for the foreseeable future. For some, this raises a terrifying specter: a world of ubiquitous Disney theme parks, symbols of American crassness and commercialism. The prospect of Mickey Mouse (or his agent, Michael Eisner) ruling the world rightly inspires terror, but the record of Euro Disney should calm some of these fears. When this theme park opened near Paris in 1992, Disney's carefully orchestrated fanfare was spoiled by some unanticipated sour notes. Some French commentators pronounced it a "cultural Chernobyl" and "a terrifying giant's step toward world homogenization."[29]

Euro Disney got off to a terrible start. Disney had overrated its innate appeal and underestimated Europeans' resistance to this very American presence in their midst. After the park lost $1.5 billion during its first three years, Disney had to change its pricing and marketing to become more "Euro friendly." This helped; the park's fortunes improved. It was, however, less than an unblemished triumph for Disney and U.S. culture. In this case, European influence reshaped an American product. That may not happen often, but it proves that there are limits to American cultural hegemony.

In the cultural relationship between the United States and Great Britain, there are no tectonic shifts under way comparable to NATO restructuring or the rise of the European Monetary Union. The two national cultures are more complementary than competing, and even if one appears dominant at a particular time, the imbalance is likely to be fleeting. Stars of the cultural world move about, with some in ascendance and some in eclipse at any given moment. That does not mean that Sylvester Stallone is going to make anyone forget Laurence Olivier, or that *The Bridges of Madison County* will displace *Vanity Fair* on lists of great novels. Eventually, one hopes, quality asserts itself; *Pride and Prejudice* outlasts *Baywatch*.

With the language as foundation, the structure is sound. Some of the grievances Frances Trollope cited continue to exist in modern form on both sides of the Atlantic, but during the passage of the almost two centuries since she traveled in the United States, the two countries have grown closer culturally than she ever would have imagined.

CHAPTER FIVE

GETTING ALONG

Despite all the elements contributing to a close relationship between the United States and Great Britain, conflicting interests do exist. Some are grounded in general international responsibilities, some involve third parties, and some arise from specific controversies that are usually not long-lasting but are nonetheless aggravating. Getting along is not always easy.

As the sole superpower, the United States is tugged in many directions. Perceiving its responsibility to be "leadership" but not always knowing precisely what that means, the United States can prove to be of questionable reliability when an ally such as Great Britain expects help.

For example, some in Britain and in other NATO countries were mystified and angered by the sluggish U.S. response to the crisis in the Balkans in the early 1990s. Particularly irksome was the hesitancy of the Clinton administration and the American public to allow U.S. military personnel to be put at risk. Britain, among others, was ready to act, not in a foolhardy fashion, but in a way that accepted the realities of bringing fierce fighting to a halt, and with a recognition that these were professional soldiers, not schoolchildren, who were to be sent on the dangerous mission.

Such disagreements are certain to arise in the conduct of high-stakes international politics. This one soon passed; under U.S. leadership a peace agreement was hammered together, and U.S. troops joined the peacekeeping force. But the lesson was not lost on Britain and other NATO members: the post–Cold War commitment of the United States to European security extends only so far. Just how far remains open to question.

In the years ahead, Great Britain's principal conflicts in its relations with the United States will probably arise from its role in the new Europe. Despite the debates about the particulars of Britain's European Union membership, it is virtually certain that Britain will be a major player in the new economic and political structure. Particularly during the first years of the new century, British officials and private citizens will be watching closely as the EU more and more reshapes life in Europe. "Preserving sovereignty" is the catchphrase that will dominate much of Britain's political discourse as the mechanics of European cooperation develop further.

While this process goes on, the United States may seem increasingly remote. The dichotomy between focusing on relations with the United States vis-à-vis those with EU members has been visible in the Euroskeptic argument that the better course for Britain is to reinforce its ties to the United States rather than being absorbed into the EU structure. This theory is based on the notion that the transatlantic relationship is more easily managed than is dealing with EU colleagues. There is not, however, much evidence to support the notion that the EU poses a substantive threat to Britain's autonomy. If the Euroskeptics were to have their way, Britain would be in danger of being isolated, with a thriving EU to the east and an ally to the west that would tend to be more attentive to Asia and perhaps even Latin America than to Britain.

In Great Britain's daily life, Europe is far more proximate in many ways than is the United States. The Channel Tunnel symbolizes this linkage, and tangible evidence abounds: in trade, in politics, in civic discourse, and in many other ways, the affairs of continental Europe imbue British life. In the United States, on the other hand, despite the close economic ties and other links, neither Great Britain nor any other European nation makes its presence felt in that way.

The two countries pursue paths that often are parallel but also often diverge. Along these paths are bumps producing stumbles that may not seriously threaten but certainly complicate the nations' relationship.

IRELAND

Since 1820, almost 5 million Irish immigrants have come to the United States. (To put that number in perspective, today's combined population of the Irish Republic and Northern Ireland is just slightly more than 5 million.) Most of them came prior to 1940, but even in the period 1991–94, almost 50,000 more arrived. About 39 million Americans claim Irish ancestry, second only to German Americans.

These numbers give Irish Americans considerable clout in U.S. politics, particularly when one of their number, such as John Kennedy or Bill Clinton (whose mother's maiden name was Cassidy), lives in the White House. On Capitol Hill in recent years, powerful figures such as Senator Edward Kennedy and House Speaker Thomas "Tip" O'Neill have not been bashful about championing the interests of their ancestral home.

Relations between Great Britain and Ireland have always been prickly at best and bloody at their frequent worst. Since the nineteenth century, Anglo-Irish affairs have had a significant U.S. dimension because of the importance of the Irish-American vote. Even though this vote is far from being a solid bloc, especially in national elections, U.S. politicians court it diligently.

In considering the political clout of Irish Americans, some historical perspective is useful. Raymond Seitz, U.S. ambassador to Great Britain from 1991 to 1994, observed: "The Irish-American community has been influential in American politics for 150 years. But it is equally true that the nineteenth century, when our political establishment was almost wholly made up of British stock, was also the period of our greatest alienation from Britain."[1]

The Irish-American political connection today takes different forms, from generic Brit bashing by a candidate in a heavily Irish Boston district to delicate negotiating between an American president and a British prime minister about easing tensions in Northern Ireland. An example of this latter kind of influence was seen when Margaret Thatcher and Irish prime minister Garret FitzGerald, in the 1985 Anglo-Irish Agreement, established an intergovernmental conference to improve the relationship between the Irish Republic and Northern Ireland. Thatcher agreed to this partly because of the urgings of Ronald Reagan. Geoffrey Smith, in his *Reagan and Thatcher*, observed that Thatcher "would normally have been distinctly hostile to any idea of giving the government of another state a formal right to influence how part of the United Kingdom should be governed. To have rejected this arrangement, however, would have been to ignore the continued, discreet pressure from the President and the evident interest of even the most moderate Irish-American politicians."[2]

The delicacy of Irish-related matters in Anglo-American relations is illustrated well by controversies related to the Irish Republican Army (IRA). The IRA and its fund-raising operation, NORAID, have enjoyed substantial U.S. political and financial backing. Depending on who is asked, this support is for widows and orphans and mainstream political activity, or for weapons and terrorism.

Margaret Thatcher subscribes to the latter theory: "The emotions of millions of decent Irish-Americans are manipulated by Irish Republican extremists, who have been able to give a romantic respectability to terrorism that its sordid reality belies."[3] She urged an end to American support of the IRA and related groups: "It is not enough to decry individual acts of terrorism but then refuse to endorse the measures required to defeat it. That applies to American Irish who supply NORAID with money to kill British citizens."[4] President Reagan spoke to the same point in his 1985 Saint Patrick's Day statement: "We in America must make every effort to ensure that, whether knowingly or unknowingly, no material, financial, or psychological help originates from this side of the Atlantic for those who advocate and practice violence. We have intensified our efforts to ensure that the United States is not the source of guns and money for such activities."[5]

British anger about Americans' pro-IRA sympathies reached a peak when the United States seemed to be condoning terrorism by foiling Britain's efforts to track down IRA members suspected of violent offenses. Some IRA members accused of criminal activity have found safe haven in the United States. For example, IRA member Joseph Doherty in 1981 escaped from a Belfast jail, fled to the United States, and was convicted in absentia of murdering a British army officer. A U.S. federal court refused Britain's extradition request because a 1972 treaty stipulated that there was to be no extradition if the offense alleged was "of a political character." Murder with political connotations is still murder, but IRA fugitives presented themselves to U.S. judges as "freedom fighters" and so could avoid being returned to their homeland.[6]

The British were appalled by this and lobbied for a new treaty that would specify crimes for which extradition would not be denied on political grounds. A treaty containing these provisions was signed in 1985, but it was held up in the Senate, partly because it was seen as contrary to the U.S. tradition of granting political asylum, and partly because it was seen as being too pro-British and anti-Irish.[7]

In efforts to secure ratification, the treaty's list of exceptions was shortened by removing possession of firearms and conspiracy from the list of crimes that could not be classified as "political offenses."[8] Probably the principal impetus for the treaty's final approval was Margaret Thatcher's support of the U.S. attack on Libya in April 1986. This led to President Reagan becoming personally involved in pushing through the treaty that Thatcher wanted so badly. He devoted one of his weekly radio addresses to this topic, saying that rejection of the treaty "would be an affront" to Thatcher, who had "at great political risk, stood shoulder to shoulder with us" during the Libyan operation.[9]

When the extradition treaty won Senate approval, so too did a measure providing about $30 million a year for the International Fund for Ireland, which was conceived during Jimmy Carter's presidency as a way to promote job creation and human rights initiatives in Northern Ireland.[10] Such issue juggling is necessary for U.S. politicians interested in supporting what they consider to be a legitimate British interest, but who are also sensitive to the political realities of Irish-American lobbying and voting clout.

Extradition and related issues continue to be part of diplomatic maneuvering. In September 1997, the Clinton administration suspended deportation action against six IRA members who had served time in British prisons for terrorist acts. The U.S. decision was clearly a payoff to Sinn Fein, the political counterpart of the IRA, for formally endorsing nonviolence. Protestant leaders in Northern Ireland, however, decried the U.S. decision, arguing that the IRA remained a terrorist organization and that the United States should not implicitly sanction IRA tactics.[11]

Sometimes the pursuit of votes based on Irish issues becomes particularly heavy-handed. In New York, for example, a statute was passed by the state legislature and signed by Governor George Pataki requiring not only that study of the nineteenth-century Irish famine be included in school curricula, but that the famine be depicted as genocide, with the British as the perpetrators. When Pataki signed the bill, he said that "the great Irish hunger was not the result of a massive failure of the Irish potato crop but, rather, was the result of a deliberate campaign by the British to deny the Irish people the food they needed to survive."[12]

Several other federal and state measures have also embraced this approach to teaching public school students about the famine. British offi-

cials have little to say on the record about such matters, but privately
they call them "sensational and emotive," "obstructions to constructive
measures," and "pandering to an ethnic voting bloc."

Far larger issues arose during Bill Clinton's first term, when U.S.
involvement (or, some would say, meddling) in Irish affairs became
particularly assertive. During the 1992 campaign, Clinton wooed Irish-
American voters by promising policy changes. In a campaign letter
sent to these voters several weeks before the election, Clinton made
his pitch:

> I believe the appointment of a special U.S. envoy to Northern Ire-
> land could be a catalyst in the effort to secure a lasting peace. We
> believe that the British government must do more to oppose job
> discrimination that has created unemployment rates two-and-a-half
> times higher for Catholic workers than Protestant workers. . . . The
> MacBride Principles set forth appropriate guidelines. . . . We also
> believe that the British government should establish more effective
> safeguards against the wanton use of lethal force and against further
> collusion between the security forces and Protestant paramilitary
> groups.[13]

As appealing as such rhetoric might be to some Irish Americans, it was
not well received by British officials. They particularly objected to the
notions that Great Britain was engaged in "wanton use of lethal force"
or had been in "collusion" with Protestant paramilitary groups. The Mac-
Bride Principles cited by Clinton are another irritant. The British say that
their law incorporates adequate antidiscrimination rules and that another
layer of guidelines is a disincentive to investment. This view is shared in
Northern Ireland by some labor unions and the Social Democratic and
Labour party (a relatively moderate Catholic/nationalist organization),
while support for the MacBride rules comes from the more militant Sinn
Fein as well as from some other groups that see the need for more antidiscrimination pressure.

The worst Ireland-related strains on Anglo-American relations came
in 1994 when Clinton ordered that Gerry Adams, the leader of Sinn
Fein, be granted a temporary visa (which had previously been denied) so
he could make a forty-eight-hour visit to the United States. The internal
debate about this action illustrated how divisive Irish issues can be.
Within the U.S. government, the visa was opposed by the attorney general, the secretary of state, the Federal Bureau of Investigation (FBI) di-

rector, the CIA director, and the U.S. ambassador to London. Supporting it were Senator Edward Kennedy, Nancy Soderberg (a former Kennedy staff member who had moved on to a top job on the National Security Council staff), and, most important, national security adviser Tony Lake. Clinton thought that granting the visa might pull Sinn Fein into peace talks and push the IRA toward a cease-fire. "We didn't come here to sit around like potted plants," Clinton told Lake. "If we have a chance to move this thing forward, we have to take it."[14]

Roderic Lyne, John Major's foreign policy adviser, telephoned Lake several times to say how upset the prime minister would be if the visa were granted,[15] but such objections were discounted. Soderberg later said, "We knew we would be going against Britain, but on the other hand we figured the special relationship was strong enough to weather a disagreement on Northern Ireland."[16]

Reaction from some in Great Britain showed that there were those who regarded the visa issue as more than "a disagreement." Several politicians asked how Americans would react if Great Britain invited Timothy McVeigh, perpetrator of the Oklahoma City bombing, to Buckingham Palace. Some press reaction was also strong. The *Sun* demanded that "the Yanks keep their noses out of Ulster," and the *Daily Express* said that Clinton's decision was "a coarse insult from a country we thought was our friend."[17]

To make the U.S. initiative evenhanded, the administration invited James Molyneaux, leader of the Ulster Unionist party, and the party's members of Parliament to come to Washington. This was designed to allay unionist (Protestant) fears that Clinton was tilting toward the IRA and nationalist (Catholic) positions on the future of Northern Ireland. In these matters, the key word for the unionists is "consent": they want the right to approve any change in the status quo. The members of Clinton's team were properly encouraging. Molyneaux, as he left the White House, said, "I believe that the principle of consent in Northern Ireland is now underwritten by American opinion in a very clear way for probably the first time in history."[18]

Clinton also pressed John Major to make a humanitarian gesture toward the IRA. The prime minister transferred some IRA prisoners from a British jail to one in Northern Ireland to make family visits easier. Tony Lake, meanwhile, became the voice of reassurance for the unionists, talking with them about a forthcoming IRA cease-fire and promising that the White House would monitor progress. To help repair damage done to the Clinton-Major relationship when the Adams visa was granted, the president told Major, for public consumption, that the cease-fire was "testi-mony to your political courage."[19] The quiet orchestration by Clinton and Lake of efforts to work through the Irish conundrum was an example of how the president saw at least one facet of his evolving post–Cold War role: leader as broker.

In addition to the low-key efforts at the White House, Clinton made his commitment to Irish peace a keystone of his December 1995 trip to Great Britain and Ireland. When he visited Belfast, tens of thousands of Catholics and Protestants gathered to hear him urge reconciliation. A widely published photograph from this occasion showed Clinton and Gerry Adams shaking hands.

In his speech at Guild Hall Square in Londonderry (or Derry, as is favored by the city's Catholic majority and as Clinton referred to it in his remarks), the president reviewed his efforts during the preceding three years:

> I have had occasion to meet with Nationalists and to meet with Unionists, and to listen to their sides of the story. I have come to the conclusion that here, as in so many other places in the world—from the Middle East to Bosnia—the divisions that are most im-portant here are not the divisions between opposing views or op-posing interests. Those divisions can be reconciled. The deep divisions, the most important ones, are those between the peace-makers and the enemies of peace—those who deep, deep down in-side want peace more than anything, and those who deep, deep down inside can't bring themselves to reach out for peace. Those who are in the ship of peace, and those who would sink it. Those who bravely meet on the bridge of reconciliation, and those who would blow it up.[20]

The following day, in a speech to the Irish Parliament in Dublin, Clinton praised the Irish Republic for its work in the peace process. He pledged to "continue our support—political, financial, and moral—to those who take risks for peace."[21]

Through this visit and the White House–orchestrated diplomacy, Clin-ton was not only intervening in the Anglo-Irish relationship, he was taking the lead. In an analysis piece for the *New York Times*, James Clarity wrote of the Northern Ireland visit: "Mr. Clinton managed to refocus attention on the overall goal of peace by speaking eloquently and force-fully over the heads of the politicians and paramilitary leaders, whose wrangling over details had slowed the peace effort to a halt in recent months." Also, wrote Clarity, "Mr. Clinton persuaded Prime Minister John Major to change London's long-held policy that the United States should have no direct role in Northern Ireland."[22]

The process Clinton introduced was a "twin-track" approach: an international commission chaired by former U.S. senator George Mitchell would address disarmament of the IRA, while the British government would hold talks with all Northern Ireland parties. Getting the major players to agree to try this was a significant accomplishment in itself. In practice, the effort predictably has had its ups and downs, particularly when violence has sporadically erupted.

British officials had, as of mid-1997, split opinions about the U.S. involvement. Some thought that Clinton had usefully co-opted Adams by giving him enhanced international stature and so forcing him to act more carefully. Knowing that the price of continued U.S. backing was IRA forbearance, Adams had reason to be a moderating influence on his nationalist colleagues.[23] Former Foreign Secretary Douglas Hurd said that the Clinton effort "began in a rather ill-thought-out way," but that the president's visit to Ireland and Mitchell's efforts both had been "big successes." "On balance," said Hurd, "it has been helpful."[24]

Prime Minister Tony Blair, whose first official trip after taking office was to Northern Ireland, made it clear that he did not expect "to see Northern Ireland as anything but a part of the United Kingdom." He also pledged to continue to work for peace and to support George Mitchell's approach.[25] Blair promptly sent his Northern Ireland secretary, Mo Mowlam, to Washington to urge the Clinton administration to keep pressure on all parties to the peace talks. Help from the White House was also requested in the effort to get an IRA cease-fire. For his part, Clinton, during his May 1997 visit to London, made it clear that the United States would not back away. He said, "Again I urge the IRA to lay down their guns for good," and he praised Blair's initial efforts to push the peace process along.

Not everyone applauds U.S. efforts. Charles Powell, who served as foreign policy adviser to Prime Ministers Thatcher and Major, said that U.S. policy "has provided aid and comfort to the IRA" and "did absolutely nothing" to resolve problems.[26] Even U.S. ambassador to London William Crowe was ambivalent. He said in 1997 that the United States "should stay out of the damn problem unless we're sure we can make a contribution." He remained pessimistic about the chances for peace, saying of the Irish factions: "They are still tribal. Everyone wants peace but only on their own terms. No one wants to compromise." He also said that one useful role being performed by the United States was to encourage investment in Northern Ireland. Crowe cited advice he had received early in his tenure in London: "If you think you understand the Ireland problem, it hasn't been explained to you right."[27]

In addition to its diplomatic initiatives, the United States has provided economic support to Northern Ireland: $1.65 billion in investment since 1991. U.S. trade missions visit Northern Ireland regularly, and if a reasonable level of peace can be maintained, more investment will follow.

Also, Bill Clinton's willingness to deal with Gerry Adams was adopted by Tony Blair, who met with Adams in Belfast in October and at 10 Downing Street in December 1997. This was the first visit of an Irish republican leader to the prime minister's official residence since Michael Collins came to see David Lloyd George in 1921.

Despite this merging of U.S. and British approaches to Northern Ireland issues, tensions remain. Among Britons, wariness about the Clinton administration's policy is reasonable, because the United States has intruded into what is fundamentally a matter of domestic politics. The assertiveness of the Clinton initiative underscores the closeness and complexity of Anglo-American ties. Clinton has forged ahead in a way that would be unthinkable in other contexts, such as the long-standing dispute between the Spanish government and Basque nationalists. The invitation to Gerry Adams, in particular, directly contravened British policy at the time toward Sinn Fein. That Clinton's judgment apparently was correct and was useful in pushing negotiations forward does not wholly overcome British resentment about the interference.

Concerns about U.S. involvement were set aside when the Belfast Agreement of April 1998 was signed, giving Northern Ireland a realistic chance to build a lasting peace. President Clinton had been actively involved in the final stages of the talks, conferring by telephone with his emissary George Mitchell, British prime minister Tony Blair, Irish prime minister Bertie Ahern, Ulster Unionist party leader David Trimble, Gerry Adams, and John Hume. Clinton assured all parties that the United States would support them if they took the political risks necessary to finalize the agreement. Clinton's intervention was particularly important in keeping Adams from walking out of the talks. As had been the case in 1994 when Adams was granted a U.S. visa, Clinton's backing gave Adams leverage in dealing with pressure from his more militant Sinn Fein colleagues.

The Belfast Agreement in itself cannot ensure the peace that has so

long eluded Northern Ireland, but the successful conclusion of these negotiations was evidence that Clinton's policy had merit. For the moment,
at least, the president was not being accused of meddling.

THE HELMS-BURTON ACT

The United States has found a sure way to strain a relationship: leg-
islating trade sanctions that apply not only to U.S. companies but also
to businesses in Great Britain and other nations. Among the most severe
of these is the Helms-Burton Act, technically the Cuban Liberty and
Democratic Solidarity Act of 1995, which President Clinton signed into
law in March 1996. It allows Americans who have claims for property
expropriated by the Cuban government to sue for damages in U.S. courts.
Among those who can be targeted in such suits are non-U.S. companies
that profit from businesses in Cuba that use expropriated property. In
addition, the act provides for excluding from the United States any officials of companies determined by the U.S. government to have been
engaged in such dealing. Members of these corporate officials' families
may also be kept out.

Helms-Burton is not the first such measure. After the Polish government imposed martial law in December 1981, the Reagan administration
ordered sanctions on trade with the Soviet Union. Among the targets
was the 2,800-mile-long Urengoi pipeline, which was to bring Soviet
natural gas to Western Europe. The ban was extended to cover foreign
companies making American-designed products under license. Among
the corporations that would have been hardest hit was John Brown Engineering, a British company with a contract worth about $170 million
to build turbines for the pipeline. Other British companies with more
than $100 million in contracts for the pipeline also would have been
affected.[28]

With 2,000 British jobs at stake, Prime Minister Thatcher invoked the
Protection of Trading Interests Act, under which the government could
prohibit British companies from obeying foreign legislation that would
damage British trade interests. Thatcher told the House of Commons:
"The question is whether one very powerful nation can prevent existing
contracts being fulfilled. I think it is wrong to do so."[29]

Thatcher later wrote that she told U.S. secretary of state Alexander
Haig that "the Americans had not included a grain embargo . . . because
this would clearly hurt their own people. Indeed few of the measures
adopted by the United States would have any serious effect at home—

but they would hurt Europe. To say the least there was a certain lack of symmetry."[30] When George Shultz became secretary of state later in 1982, he allowed existing contracts for the pipeline to proceed. This satisfied the British, but Thatcher later said that "it had all been a lesson in how not to conduct alliance business."[31]

The high-handedness that concerned Thatcher is seen again in Helms-Burton. Aiming at Fidel Castro, an ever-popular political target, Congress and the White House not only threatened U.S. companies and their foreign subsidiaries, but also tried to muscle other nations, especially Canada and Spain, that were expanding their investments in Cuba.

British trade and industry minister Ian Taylor said in May 1996 that Helms-Burton "follows some bad precedents in seeking to impose U.S. law on transactions involving third parties and it would be thoroughly unwelcome on those grounds alone. . . . We believe that the way to bring Cuba into the global community is through trade and investment, not isolation." Noting the Helms-Burton provision banning certain corporate officials' family members from the United States, Taylor brought some nice pathos to the controversy when he said that the measure could be used "to ban a five-year-old child from visiting Disneyland."[32]

In October 1996, the European Union enacted a "clawback" measure that would allow member nations' companies to countersue U.S. companies in their own countries' courts to recover anything lost in U.S. courts under Helms-Burton. (Canada enacted similar legislation.) The United States was also threatened with requests by the EU that the World Trade Organization (WTO) declare illegal the extraterritorial provisions of Helms-Burton.

By mid-1997, the EU and the United States were searching for compromise. The Americans had argued that Helms-Burton was a national security measure, not a trade issue, and therefore was outside the WTO's jurisdiction. That argument, however, undercuts the authority of the WTO, which the United States has long wanted to police openness in global trade and investment. The EU's chief trade negotiator, Sir Leon Brittan of Great Britain, tried to give the Clinton administration some room for maneuvering by offering to have the EU push Cuba toward liberalization and to bar future investments in properties expropriated by the Castro government. For his part, President Clinton deferred enforcement of the U.S. law. In April 1998, as part of this diplomatic minuet, the European Union dropped its formal legal challenge to the Helms-Burton Act. The Clinton administration, meanwhile, indicated it would continue to avoid enforcing the measure. Both sides, however, indicated that the matter had not yet been finally resolved.

Seeking to annoy Castro is a well-established U.S. political sport, especially popular during election years. Clinton's acquiescence to the Helms-Burton Act had more to do with his hopes for carrying Florida in the 1996 presidential race than with his expectations of doing any substantial harm to Cuba. But the real damage was done to U.S. relations with its allies, including Great Britain. More significant than the financial problems the law might cause was the perceived bullying behind the statute—the assumption by U.S. policy makers that their word is, literally, law. As Ian Taylor said: "The United States has the right to conduct its foreign policy in the light of its own convictions. The United Kingdom is not, however, obliged to follow its lead."[33] This is a simple but important message. The United States would do well to heed it.

DOMESTIC POLITICS

Given the closeness of the Anglo-American relationship, political leaders in both countries occasionally succumb to the temptation to dabble in the politics of the moment on the opposite side of the Atlantic. If one is on the winner's side, all will be well, but backing the wrong horse and losing the bet can prove very costly.

During the 1992 U.S. presidential election, George Bush and Bill Clinton received assistance from, respectively, Britain's Conservative and Labour parties. In the midst of the campaign, the right-leaning Heritage Foundation brought top Tory campaign officials John Lacy and Mark Fulbrook to Washington to brief the Bush-Quayle campaign staff and the Republican National Committee about how John Major, despite a recession and voters' unhappiness with the long-in-power Conservatives, had been able to win the British general election in April of that year. Their message was heeded. According to journalist Martin Walker, "Bush television ads began running showing snapshots of families, individuals, and elderly couples, each with a sum, ranging into thousands of dollars, which was allegedly what Clinton's tax plans would cost them. It was a direct copy of the Conservative ads in the British tabloids in April."[34]

For their part, the Democrats enlisted the help of Philip Gould, who had been communications and polling director for Labour's campaign. He came to Little Rock to work with strategist James Carville and others in the Clinton war room. When Republicans attempted to create a scandal

about Clinton's 1969 student trip to Moscow, Gould provided background information about similar Tory attacks on Labour party leader
Neil Kinnock because he had visited the Soviet embassy in London.[35]

The Clinton team effectively countered the tax ads with its own television spots, and criticism of Clinton's Moscow visit did little damage.
A number of the Conservative operatives' suggestions were so absurd that
even the desperate Bush campaign refused to implement them. One British idea was to put up billboards with Gennifer Flowers's picture and the
slogan, "And now he wants to screw the whole country." Another proposal was to circulate a faked photograph of Clinton that would depict
him as a long-haired hippy with a Mao jacket and a Vietcong flag.[36]

These efforts might have been dismissed as standard campaign silliness
and soon forgotten, but some British officials, in their eagerness to see
Bush reelected, went even farther. They perused the 1968–70 files in the
British Home Office to see if they could find any damaging reports about
Clinton's activities while he had been a student at Oxford.[37] This was
more an official government act than a free-lance political venture, and
it did not help the Clinton-Major relationship when the new president
took office. U.S. Speaker of the House Tom Foley said of this incident,
"The British meddling was outrageous and I think it went very deep with
Clinton."[38]

Political cross-pollination continued during the Clinton administration, with the Democrats serving as mentors of sorts for the rebuilding
Labour party and its new leader, Tony Blair. Just as Clinton had targeted
the political middle by running as a "New Democrat," Blair portrayed
himself as the exponent of "New Labour."

Blair's fascination with Clinton's accomplishment was controversial in
some Labour circles, fueling the argument between modernizers and tra-
ditionalists in the party. This was particularly the case when Blair seemed
to be positioning himself as a centrist and began sounding very much like
Clinton. In May 1993, for example, Blair said:

> We play the Tory game when we say we've got to speak up for the
> underclass rather than the broad majority of people in this country.
> It's not just an electoral fact that you will lose an election if you
> allow yourself to be painted into that corner, though you will. . . .
> What we have got to do is to show how, by giving those people
> opportunity, we actually assist the whole of society to prosper.[39]

This appeal to a broad and moderate "middle England" electorate ech-
oed the Clinton rhetoric of 1992. Although Blair dislikes being charac-

terized as a Clinton clone, his repositioning of Labour in preparation for the 1997 campaign was much like Clinton's strategy: move the party rightward, exile the radicals, and offer voters a nonthreatening centrism. This shrewd transformation of Labour, coupled with public disenchantment with the Tories, helped produce the Blair-led Labour landslide.

George Bush getting pointers about how John Major turned a weak campaign into a winner and Tony Blair learning about the joys of centrism from Bill Clinton are logical bridges between political systems that have much in common. Usually, no harm is done. When, however, the sharing of information gives way to official involvement, as was the case in the British investigation of Clinton's Oxford activities, considerable damage may result. A foreign government—no matter that it is a friendly one—is trying to influence an election outcome. There is something intrinsically arrogant about that. It is a sure way to undermine a valuable relationship.

Since Labour's victory, party leaders' relations with the Clinton administration have been close. In November 1997, members of the Blair government met at Chequers, the prime minister's official country residence, with Hillary Clinton and a number of Clinton advisers to discuss "the progressive agenda." This session was just one instance of a renewed policy-shaping partnership between political leaders of the two countries. When Chancellor of the Exchequer Gordon Brown granted independence to the Bank of England, he reportedly did so after conversations with U.S. Federal Reserve Board chairman Alan Greenspan and Deputy Secretary of the Treasury Lawrence Summers. These connections are evidence, noted *The Economist*, that "intellectually, the British government is still a lot closer to America than to Europe."[40]

OTHER PLAYERS

Part of the strength of the Anglo-American relationship has been the implicit primacy that has been attached to it by both parties. These are not just friends, they are best friends.

The realities of geopolitics, however, do not encourage exclusivity. Great Britain must deal with European and other partners in ways not necessarily in the interest of the United States, and the United States likewise will sometimes see its interests best advanced by building relationships that supersede the one with Great Britain. As part of day-to-day business, political leaders understand the necessity of flexible and diverse allegiances, but they also may become wary when they suspect that an ally's temporary arrangements with a third party are becoming longer-lasting. How the United States and Great Britain deal with other nations will inevitably affect how they get along with each other.

Germany

The inherent strength and historical menace of Germany unfailingly worry its European neighbors. Even when other nations discount the likelihood of the reemergence of behavior rooted in Germany's horrific past, they know that Germany could easily become too dominant for their comfort. It also could be a major contributor to a lasting peace on the Continent. Vaclav Havel has said, "The relationship of Germany to the family of European nations, and of this family to Germany—if only because of its size, strength, and central position—have traditionally been the most important element of European stability."[41]

Germans themselves view the future through glasses tinted by the past. They recognize their innate power and grapple with the problem of using it in constructive, nonthreatening ways. Former German chancellor Helmut Schmidt has written: "After losing two world wars and constraining itself within a web of European institutions, Germany will never again become a world power." He adds a note of caution: "Since reunification, Germany's population is over 80 million, almost one-and-a-half times that of Britain or France and double that of Poland. Germany's preponderance in Europe poses a potential threat to the stability of the continent, and it must be bound into Europe-wide institutions."[42] Havel and Schmidt recognize, as do many others, that German actions will do much to determine if "European stability" is to be real or illusory.

Germany continues to mature, and it no longer should be dismissed as merely "an economy in search of political purpose," which is how Henry Kissinger described it when President Richard Nixon visited there in 1969.[43] Germany is, however, still in search of its role in Europe and the world. About Germany's apparent indecisiveness, American scholar Tony Judt observed, "German politicians from Adenauer to Helmut Kohl had made a point of playing down German strength, deferring to French political initiatives, and emphasizing their own wish for nothing more than a stable Germany in a prosperous Europe; they have thus fallen victim to their own rhetoric, bequeathing to post-1989 Europe a muscle-bound state with no sense of national purpose."[44] In the almost thirty years between Kissinger's and Judt's observations, Germany has unquestionably grown stronger, but its place in Europe remains incompletely defined.

Despite having led alliances against Germany in two world wars, the United States is relatively relaxed in its appraisals of how Germany will wield its strength. Of course, unlike many European nations, the United States has never had German bombs drop on its soil. Also, the United States has viewed the fundamentally strong German economy as a contributor to widespread prosperity, not a means to achieve unwelcome dominance.

This U.S. attitude has seemed to some in Europe, particularly in Great Britain, simplistically sunny. For example, Margaret Thatcher took umbrage when George Bush in a 1989 speech referred to the Germans as "partners in leadership." This, she wrote in her memoirs, "confirmed the way American thinking about Europe was going."[45] Thatcher attributed Bush's position to his secretary of state, James Baker, whose pragmatism did not always sit well with her. The main results of Baker's approach, she wrote, "were to put the relationship with Germany—rather than the 'special relationship' with Britain—at the center. I would be the first to argue that if one chose to ignore history and the loyalties it engenders, such an approach might appear quite rational."[46]

The basis for Thatcher's sensitivity about what she saw as Bush's and Baker's tilt toward Germany is reflected in her observations about the European balance of power:

> When, in pursuit of its own interests, a state allies with other states to counter and contain a regional power which threatens to become dominant, a generally beneficial equilibrium is achieved: and temptations and opportunities for misbehavior are reduced. It was, of course, British policy for many years to promote such a balance of power within Europe; and . . . this still makes sense when a major, if unstated, objective of policy should be the containment of German power.[47]

"Containment" recalls the West's assertive Cold War strategy for dealing with the Soviet Union and, as such, implies a forcefulness that is not needed in relations with Germany today. Thatcher's caution is, however, useful in offsetting any nonchalance in dealing with the Germans. Even those who place little value on the lessons of history must recognize Germany's intrinsic power, no matter how dormant it may be.

Nervousness about Germany is not limited to Great Britain. Neighbors such as Poland will always watch Germany warily, while Russia may be the most concerned about German resurgence. The two countries have a long history of enmity, and Russia, which lost 20 million of its people during World War II, worries about the prospect of Germany becoming more dominant within NATO. Thomas Mann noted the desirability of "a Europeanized Germany, not a Germanized Europe." That principle remains popular among many of today's European leaders.

The United States is the stabilizing force that fosters the continued equilibrium that Thatcher advocates. If the United States were to withdraw or even substantially reduce its European presence, Germany might be tempted to do more to take care of its own security.

What "doing more" means is open to question. In a Europe without active U.S. involvement, Britain and France (as nuclear powers) might see themselves as the principal guardians of European security, but Germany might not consider an Anglo-French shield to be adequate. During the Cold War, being able to rely on the U.S. nuclear umbrella let the nations of Western Europe avoid serious jockeying for security-related leadership positions. Flags were waved occasionally—by the French, for instance—but everyone, including the Warsaw Pact states, knew that the United States was the ultimate guarantor of Western Europe's security.

Maintaining that status quo today seems of lesser value to the United States than it does to most Europeans. The massive costs of even a reduced U.S. military presence may not be politically sustainable indefinitely. As the U.S. security role in Europe shrinks, Britain wants to establish its own position as leader and as protector of its own interests and not be pushed aside by U.S. policy that shoves Germany to the forefront.

The Germans, meanwhile, are quietly expanding their military role within NATO. In Bosnia, the Bundeswehr is participating in the Stabilization Force (SFOR), deploying 3,000 servicemen. The core of this contingent is an armored unit that is Germany's contribution to a joint Franco-German brigade. German defense minister Volker Ruhe cites "a new and wide-ranging consensus in Germany" in support of this effort, noting that this involvement represents "a sea change in German security policy."[48]

The U.S.-German relationship also continues to evolve. Protecting Germany was an important domestic political issue in the United States during the Cold War, but no longer. Germany's dependence on U.S.-led NATO for protection is also no longer so important. As NATO expands, Germany will have an eastern buffer between it and Russia, and in any event it faces no danger comparable to the now-vanished threat of a Soviet invasion.

Germany's top priorities are EU related, which means that making deals with Paris may be more important than courting Washington. About this, former Chancellor Schmidt writes:

> Germany remains thankful to the United States for the help and encouragement it received throughout the Cold War, and America can rely on this gratitude. On the other hand, the United States must understand that in the next century Germany will not automatically take its side in disputes between Washington and Paris. Germany's vital interest dictates that it not become isolated or insulated from its European neighbors, and France is most important.[49]

Although security concerns may seem highly speculative absent a true threat to Europe, Great Britain is more specifically worried about an ascendant Germany having too much influence on the workings of the European Union. In a speech in Bonn in February 1997, Foreign Secretary Malcolm Rifkind presented some of Britain's concerns. He was careful to wrap his criticisms in gentle language, citing the two nations' shared commitment to open markets and saying that when he pointed out differences, "I hope you will understand that I am doing so as a partner, a friend, and a fellow European."

At the heart of Britain's concern, as expressed by Rifkind, is wariness about movement toward a United States of Europe—a federal entity that would erode the autonomy of its member nations. Although Helmut Kohl has officially kept his distance from the notion of a unified European state, Rifkind cited a number of German proposals Britain has found troubling: a common electoral system for choosing members of the European Parliament; jurisdictional supremacy for the European Court of Justice; common defense and police mechanisms; and an overall trend toward centralized European authority over legal and social policy. "People in Britain and in other countries," said Rifkind, "would not accept being overruled" on social policy issues related to housing, schools, and health. "Why do people accept being overruled in national parliaments but not at the level of the European Union? It is because while they feel part of a European culture they do not feel themselves to be part of a single European nation."[50] In this passage is the essence of the "Eurocaution" that characterizes British policy about the EU. It is Thatcherist wariness, modified somewhat by John Major. It also reflects persistent skepticism about German motives.

In addition to trying to influence the evolution of the EU, Germany is playing its own game in Central Europe. There, economic dependence on the former Soviet Union is an unpleasant but fading memory; by early 1997, two-thirds of the trade of Poland, Hungary, and the Czech Republic was with the EU, and half of that was with Germany.[51] Given the EU's currency and agricultural policies (among other factors), early admission to the EU will prove a challenge for even the healthiest of the former Communist states. For all parties, the best deal at the moment is active trade without formal ties of membership. Germany, by virtue of geography and assertive policy making, has made itself the principal beneficiary of this trade.

Neither Great Britain nor other EU members have much ground for complaint about this. After all, the dominant philosophy of post–Cold War Europe is "Trade is good, and more trade is better." For the moment, Germany's windfall has its limits; Eastern European economic health is robust only when compared to its status during the Soviet-bloc years. Over the long haul, however, Germany's efficient construction of trade linkages with its eastern neighbors will probably pay significant dividends. The extent to which Germany monopolizes that trade and exerts, through heavy investment, influence on the developing economic policy of these newly capitalist nations could affect the overall balance of wealth in twenty-first-century Europe. Tony Blair, in his speeches prior to becoming prime minister, acknowledged German economic achievements and implicitly endorsed a leadership combination of Great Britain, Germany, and France as Europe's future takes shape.[52]

Currently and prospectively, Germany is so strong that there is little sense in not recognizing that a powerful, perhaps dominant, Germany will continue to be a fact of European life. That this is a fact, however, does not necessarily make it palatable. The politics of memory is at work in Great Britain and elsewhere. Despite the progressive rhetoric from all quarters, Germany does not write on a clean slate. The United States may not be as sensitive to this as some other countries are, but it should be taken into consideration in evaluating the outlook of Great Britain and other European allies.

France

Although Great Britain has been willing to shake hands with Germany, France has embraced the Germans in a robust Gallic hug. Tony Judt has said of this, "The unspoken premise of France's relations with West Germany was this: you pretend not to be powerful and we'll pretend not to

notice that you are."[53] Margaret Thatcher has predicted that this relationship will become uncomfortable for France as Germany becomes the
increasingly dominant partner, and that the French may come to find
Britain a more agreeable friend. She writes: "It should not be beyond the
capacity of a future British prime minister to rebuild an Anglo-French
entente as a counter-balance to German influence."[54]

From their perspective, the French have various reasons for courting
the Germans:

- The desire to keep Germany a collegial partner rather than an unpredictable loner.
- The expectation that Germany will dominate the EU economy and that
  its best friends will benefit most from this domination.
- The assumption that U.S. influence in the new Europe will shrink and
  that a Franco-German team can fill the resulting leadership gap.

Whatever the rationale, more is involved than simple bilateral affection.
France remains dedicated to its perpetual mission to assert itself as a leader
in Europe and the world. That quest helps shape its relationships with
the United States and Great Britain, and in turn affects Anglo-American
ties.

France is seen by the British as being a major proponent of faster and
more thorough European integration. This is related to the Franco-
German relationship. The roots of today's EU are to be found in the
efforts of two Frenchmen, Jean Monnet and Robert Schuman, to bring
about post–World War II reconciliation between France and Germany
through creation of the European Coal and Steel Community. As this
institution evolved into the Common Market during the 1950s, Great
Britain was more observer than player, reluctant to plunge into uncharted
waters. Monnet said of this: "You British always find it difficult to accept
principles and prefer to make your decisions on the basis of facts. We on
the continent first set out the principles, believing that the facts will
emerge later."[55] During the 1960s, when Great Britain belatedly tried to
join the Common Market, French president Charles de Gaulle vetoed
the bid, partly because he thought that the British had forfeited their
right to participate by delaying and not sharing risks, and partly because
he believed that they were too closely tied to the Americans.

Today, the French are vocal supporters of promptly developing the
EU's own foreign and security policies. Britain is again cautious, less

averse to the substance of French goals than to the pace that the French
have tried to set. In all these dealings, the complicated aspirations of the
French are matched by the equally complicated way the French view their
allies. De Gaulle was always wary of the Americans and the British. He
considered France to be an ally of the United States only in a limited,
pragmatic way, and he felt that France needed to be liberated from the
influence of the Anglo-Saxons.[56] Nicholas Henderson, former British ambassador to France (and also the British ambassador to Germany and to
the United States) is among those who have noted that "the French had
a 'Trojan horse' fixation" about the British, fearing that Britain "would
insinuate unwanted American ideas or influence into the European
camp."[57]

Henderson cites advice he was given by a French diplomat before he
began his ambassadorship in Paris: "Every day you are in France, do not
forget two facts: firstly, that we had a Revolution, such as you never had;
secondly, that we were defeated in 1940, and you were not. You will find
these facts relevant in all your dealings with the French."[58] The British
have sometimes ignored such advice and made obvious their impatience
with the French. When Prime Minister Thatcher was invited to France
during the bicentennial celebration of the French Revolution, she compared France's experience unfavorably to England's Glorious Revolution
of 1688, which she noted was "a quiet revolution, where Parliament ex-
erted its will over the King." She also said: "Human rights did not begin
with the French Revolution. . . . 'Liberty, equality, fraternity'—they for-
got obligations and duties, I think. And then, of course, the fraternity
went missing for a long time."[59] The remarks were quintessential
Thatcher, and the French were not pleased.

Thatcher's abrasiveness on this matter was not out of step with British
public opinion. A 1996 MORI (Market and Opinion Research International) poll found that 8 percent of Britons considered France, among
European Union nations, to be Great Britain's "most reliable political
ally," trailing only Germany, which was so designated by 15 percent of
the respondents. But in the category of "least reliable political ally,"
France was named by 50 percent of respondents; Germany was a distant
second at 14 percent.[60] Across the Atlantic, a 1994 poll conducted by
the Chicago Council on Foreign Relations found that U.S. respondents
tended to have neutral feelings about France, giving it a 55 rating, compared to 69 for Great Britain and 57 for Germany. (In this "temperature"
survey, 50 "degrees" was neutral; warm feelings were those above 50, cool
feelings those below it.)[61]

The United States remains wary of French maneuvering, particularly in security matters. The Gulf War proved that France does not have the military ability to back up its military aspirations. Its conventional capabilities are outdated, and its nuclear weapons are of questionable relevance in a Europe under no nuclear threat. Even if such a threat were to evolve, the United States, not France or, for that matter, Great Britain, certainly would be looked to once again as the guarantor of European security. Unless the United States declined that role—a hardly imaginable response—France would find itself still merely a supporting player.

In dealing with France, the 1986 observations of Nicholas Henderson are worth remembering:

> It is impossible to live in France today or do international business with the French without being reminded frequently of the glory of France, of its civilizing mission for other countries. . . . What struck me often in Paris was the preoccupation with the concept of France, the self-consciousness about France and what it stood for, which was never anything mean or small or insignificant to others, but indeed something from which everyone stood to benefit. In one quite short speech, [President] Giscard [d'Estaing] used the word "France" over twenty times.[62]

For Great Britain and the United States, France remains something of a paradox—an ally, to be sure, but one that likes to maintain an arm's-length relationship. In the eyes of U.S. policy makers, France's unpredictability makes Great Britain look even better. Although France lacks Germany's economic clout and the German vantage point as gateway to Eastern Europe, the French will remain strong enough to retain a central role in shaping Europe's future, casting their shadow on Anglo-American relations.

After the June 1997 French election, that shadow may tilt leftward for a while. The Socialist-led coalition derives part of its strength from its unwillingness to let EU priorities—particularly EMU membership requirements—supersede France's domestic social agenda. France certainly will not be the last EU member to experience such political volatility. This is the kind of detour that the EU should anticipate and address with equanimity. A detour delays, but need not prevent, reaching the ultimate destination.

Meanwhile, from the U.S. standpoint, Great Britain seems by comparison to be a bastion of stability. It is predictable (in a positive sense) and lacks the residual anti-Americanism that, even if it is mild, continues to influence French foreign policy. France zigzags; Britain holds to a more consistent course. The United States values the latter.

Canada

As is the case with the United States, much of Canada's heritage is rooted in British soil. Although a primary issue in Canada today is the tension between English- and French-speaking parts of the country, the nation remains closely tied to Britain. A member of the British Commonwealth, Canada, says British professor Beatrice Heuser, "is still thought of as an extension of Britain itself, the place of refuge in catastrophe, a country with which British leaders are happy to share most secret intelligence data and analysis."[63]

Over the years, Canada has reciprocated, proving itself a dependable partner. In the Boer War, 7,000 Canadian volunteers fought alongside British troops; 600,000 Canadians volunteered in World War I; more than 1 million Canadians were under arms during World War II; and Canadian troops were stationed in Europe throughout the Cold War.[64]

Immigration figures also illustrate Canada's ties to Britain. In 1994, for example, about 39,000 immigrants to Canada—approximately 18 percent of the year's total—came from Great Britain or British territories. Fewer than 2,800 came from France.[65]

In security and economic matters, Canada sometimes serves as a bridge between the United States and Europe. Beatrice Heuser writes: "Canada is strangely poised between the two continents, like the United States a child of Europe, but unlike it one that has never rejected its parents and has only half-heartedly left home. Canadians see themselves almost as Europeans, and their greatest disappointment seems to be that Europeans do not give them as much attention as they give to one another or to Canada's big North American neighbor."[66] Sometimes fearing that their identity has been overwhelmed by that of the United States, Canadians have tried to develop closer ties of their own to Europe (as, for example, during Pierre Trudeau's tenure as prime minister), but the realities of geography have frustrated that effort.

Despite its real and perceived closeness to the United States, Canada is not considered a second-string player. Its economic muscle has made it a member of the G-7. (The G-7, or Group of Seven, comprises the major economic powers: Canada, France, Germany, Great Britain, Italy,

Japan, and the United States.) Recognizing that a stable Europe is essential to Canadian as well as U.S. security, the Canadians have been important contributors to NATO.

The politics of Canada's role in NATO has sometimes been complex, illustrating the duality of being closely tied to Europe without being truly European. NATO participation has been seen by some as a kind of dues paying by the Canadians to ensure their role in European policy-making circles. For instance, during the 1970s, German chancellor Helmut Schmidt made it clear that the success of Canada's efforts to improve trade with the European Community would be contingent on Canada renewing its commitments to NATO.[67] At the same time, Canadian prime minister Trudeau was trying to reduce his country's military contribution to NATO. Trudeau's effort failed. Canada stayed very much involved with NATO, and its 1976 purchase of German-made battle tanks was evidence that Schmidt's argument had prevailed.[68]

Overall, Canada has been an effective and reliable partner for both Great Britain and the United States, skillfully balancing the two relationships. The formal Commonwealth links to Great Britain cause little problem; Canada, like the United States, is one of Britain's adult children that has established a full life of its own. Meanwhile, the increasingly strong economic ties to the United States have enhanced the north-south bond.

In the politics of foreign trade, Canada always has carefully tended its interests on both sides of the Atlantic. When the thirteen colonies that were to become the United States first seceded, loyalists in Canada profited from the British commerce that was taken away from American merchants. During the Napoleonic Wars, Britain relied on Canadian timber and grain while turmoil on the Continent disrupted the flow of basic materials from European sources.[69]

During the nineteenth century, Britain was Canada's protector against American expansionism, and trade between Canada and Britain remained strong even after Britain embraced free trade in the 1840s. This continued into the twentieth century, but with World War II a dramatic turnaround in the export pattern began. In 1938, 41 percent of Canadian exports went to Great Britain, while 32 percent went to the United States. By 1953, these figures were 16 percent to Great Britain and 58 percent to the United States. In 1994, they were 2 percent to Great Britain and 82 percent to the United States. As for imports, the change in U.S. imports into Canada went only from 63 percent in 1938 to 68 percent in 1994, but imports from Great Britain dropped during those years from 18 percent to 3 percent. Increased imports from Japan made up part of the difference.[70]

Investment between the United States and Canada has also far outstripped that between Canada and Great Britain. In the mid-1990s, slightly more than 60 percent of direct foreign investment in Canada came from the United States, while Great Britain accounted for less than 20 percent. Of outgoing Canadian investment, slightly less than 60 percent went to the United States, while about 10 percent went into Great Britain.[71] It should be noted that beginning in the 1980s, the U.S. share of direct investment in Canada declined as other countries, particularly Japan, made their presence felt.[72]

According to Gregory Marchildon of Johns Hopkins University, all this activity between the United States and Canada has produced "the postwar world's largest bilateral trading and investment relationship."[73] Canada has built on this linkage by expanding its trade base to include Asian and Western European countries, in addition to Great Britain. While the United States remains the best market for Canada's manufactured goods, Japan, China, and the Europeans buy primarily natural-resource goods.[74]

With the creation of NAFTA, the North American foundation of Canadian trade became even more important. If NAFTA expands southward (as is likely to happen), the economic orientation of Canada, like that of the United States, may become directed even more toward its fellow Western Hemisphere states.

The formalities of NAFTA aside, the combined economic power of the United States and Canada constitutes a counterweight to the European Union. This makes some British Atlanticists yearn for closer ties to these former outposts of their empire. Realistically, however, ties to North America should be seen as a complement to, rather than a substitute for, Great Britain's linkage to the rest of Europe.

THE NEXT STAGE OF ANGLO-AMERICAN RELATIONS

Closeness can breed presumptuousness, and this will test any relationship, be it between individuals or nations. The U.S. excursions into the Northern Ireland peace process, for instance, feature a mix of good intentions, naïveté, and high-handedness that may leave a residue of resentment in Great Britain regardless of the outcome. Similarly, British meddling in the 1992 U.S. presidential campaign was outside the bounds of appropriate behavior between nations and created some lingering bitterness.

These examples illustrate how Anglo-American relations are not problem-free, but they also are evidence of the fundamental resilience of the partnership. With so many shared interests rooted in so much shared tradition, bad feelings exist only for a while, then dissipate. Grudges are not held for long. Equilibrium is soon restored.

Getting along may not always be easy, but it is worth the effort. The U.S.-British friendship stands above the respective relationships with other allies, such as the Germans and French. In terms of common goals and dependability, neither Great Britain nor the United States can rely on anyone else as much as they can on each other. Margaret Thatcher's formulation at the time of the 1986 U.S. bombing of Libya that "an ally is an ally" was noble but simplistic. Not all allies are alike; not all can be counted on without doubt during a crisis. The U.S.-British linkage is one of the few that can be trusted to hold firm in such circumstances.

This durability bodes well for the future. As the dynamics of geopolitics continue to change, the ability of the United States and Great Britain to get along and rely on each other will be increasingly important. Both nations' strength in dealing with the rest of the world will be enhanced by this relationship.

That does not mean, however, that the status quo will endure. Much change is under way in economic, defense, and other matters. To meet the demands this change entails, the United States and Great Britain should jointly take the lead in trying to make security and prosperity the dominant characteristics of the new century. That will be the next stage of Anglo-American relations.

CHAPTER SIX

THE NEW CENTURY

What is the outlook for the new century? Keeping the Anglo-American relationship healthy will require an ambitious agenda, even though recent measures of public opinion in the United States and Great Britain illustrate the fundamental strength of this relationship. A Gallup poll conducted in May 1994 asked Americans and Britons how reliable an ally the other country would be during a serious crisis. Of the American respondents, 88 percent rated Great Britain as "very" or "somewhat" reliable, while 87 percent of the Britons rated the United States likewise.[1] A MORI poll conducted in Britain in June 1995 asked respondents whether their attitudes were basically favorable or unfavorable toward several countries. For the United States, the answers were 66 percent favorable, 12 percent unfavorable, and the rest either neutral or no opinion. No other country listed in the survey received a higher rating. (By comparison, Germany received ratings of 49 percent favorable and 20 percent unfavorable.)[2]

Despite these positive findings, British attitudes about the importance of the relationship with the United States have been changing. Consider the answers to MORI's question "Which of these—Europe, the Commonwealth, or America—is the most important to Britain?"[3]:

	1969	1989	1993	1996
Europe	21%	50	57	45
Commonwealth	34	21	18	22
America	34	19	15	22
Don't know	11	10	10	11

The 1996 figures reflect the rise in British skepticism about the EU, but the reordering of priorities is nevertheless clear. Britons contemplating their future are looking more often across the Channel than across the Atlantic.

In a 1994 U.S. survey that asked about U.S. interests abroad, Great Britain placed seventh on the list, rated as a vital U.S. interest by 69 percent of respondents. Japan led the list, followed by Saudi Arabia, Russia, Kuwait, Mexico, and Canada.[4]

This melange of poll results illustrates the overall positive feelings that Americans and Britons have for one another, but it also underscores the need to avoid viewing the Anglo-American relationship in isolation. Much competition exists in the pursuit of attention and loyalty. Also, British feelings about the United States seem to reflect Churchill's observation that the United States ultimately does the right thing after having exhausted all other options. Robert Worcester, an American who runs the London-based MORI, says that from a British standpoint the problem with relying on the United States is that "the United States is a benign bear—half-asleep, more concerned with scratching its belly than with paying attention to the world. The problem with being in bed with a bear is you never know when it might roll over."[5]

Being in bed with a bear might also, however, have its advantages. The bear can be useful as protection against those who might think twice before tangling with such a beast. The pros and cons of a bear as a partner are among the factors creating some sensitivity about the closeness of Anglo-American ties.

In defining the status of today's Anglo-American linkage, even semantics can be important. Raymond Seitz, as he ended his tenure as U.S. ambassador to Great Britain, noted that when he first assumed the job,

> I said I would eschew the phrase "special relationship" not because
> I had any particular aversion to it, but because I felt its misty quality
> clouded what was at stake. The phrase had become too nostalgic

and backward-looking, an evocation that did not necessarily contribute to the hard thinking necessary in a new world. . . . To declare a relationship "special" does not make it so, nor does it adequately define the elements that make this relationship particularly different from any of a number of others. The phrase relies on unarticulated givens at a moment in history when all givens need reexamination.[6]

Similarly, British foreign secretary Douglas Hurd said: "I don't believe in talking about a special relationship in ways that diminish other relationships. I don't think it is like children in a schoolyard rushing up and down and saying, 'My relationship is more special than yours.' "[7]

Loud proclamations about "specialness" may be just flimsy rhetoric, but there are tangible manifestations of closeness. Hurd notes "the feeling of being a bit upstream in dealing with Washington" while he was foreign secretary—an ability to play a uniquely inside role. He cites his own visit to the White House on the day President George Bush decided to end the Persian Gulf War. Hurd says that "it just seemed natural" to be included in conversations about strategy with the president, Joint Chiefs of Staff Chairman Colin Powell, and others.[8] Hurd's experience and judgment certainly were respected within the White House, but it is unlikely that another country's foreign secretary would have been included in such sensitive discussions. Being British—and thus being "special"—made the difference.

Seitz's point about the "misty quality" of the term "special relationship" is valid, but the polling data and Hurd's account are among the evidence making clear that a "specialness" does exist in important ways. Any appraisal of the future of Anglo-American ties should include a realistic appreciation of the historic depth and day-to-day manifestations of this closeness. Despite the many ups and downs in this relationship, the United States and Great Britain will certainly move into the twenty-first century with a friendship as firm as any two nations are likely to have.

But good feelings are not enough. For instance, meeting mutual security needs—the cornerstone of the Anglo-American partnership—will demand leadership more creative than has been displayed so far. Although the Clinton administration pushed through its NATO expansion plan at the 1997 Madrid summit, it has made a less-than-compelling case for assuming the costs and responsibilities that will accompany a larger alliance. Clinton said that by approving the expansion, NATO had "erased an artificial line drawn across Europe by Stalin after the Second World War." But by drawing a new and perhaps no less artificial line, NATO risks further destabilizing the already-fragile post-Soviet Russia. The prospect of a "Weimar Russia"—bullied to the point of internal explosion or external lashing out—should not be dismissed.

Also, as NATO grows, so too do chances increase that a border dispute or similar flare-up will trigger the intervention guaranteed by the organization's charter. Sending U.S. troops as part of a NATO response to a confrontation between, for example, Hungary and Ukraine could well prove politically devastating to the president on whose watch it happened, especially if casualties were incurred.

Costs also present hazards. The Clinton White House estimates that the expansion could cost as little as $1.5 billion; the Congressional Budget Office has said that the cost could reach $125 billion. The difference between the two estimates is so large that the honesty of at least one of them should be questioned. Also, both these projections are based on the premise that NATO will not expand further during the next fifteen years, but President Clinton has implicitly promised otherwise.

All these issues are likely to prove controversial within the United States if the public pays some attention and begins asking why NATO expansion is in the interest of the United States. Meanwhile, Great Britain so far has followed the U.S. lead, supporting Clinton's insistence on initially admitting only Poland, Hungary, and the Czech Republic. Problems may arise, however, when bills come due. Although British defense contractors, as well as those in the United States and elsewhere, anticipate reaping a bonanza as the new members are brought up to NATO military standards, the Blair government has shown no enthusiasm about picking up much of the tab for expansion. If Clinton faces political heat at home about costs, he will certainly turn to other established NATO members to help out. The negotiations that will ensue could well strain Anglo-American ties.

Already, NATO expansion has exacerbated tensions between the United States and France. French president Jacques Chirac (joined by Italian prime minister Romano Prodi) strongly urged admitting two more nations, Romania and Slovenia, and grew increasingly angry about what he considered to be U.S. haughtiness. At the Denver economic summit that preceded the Madrid meeting, Clinton refused to be moved, and Chirac reportedly told his aides: "We're wasting our time here. We're nothing but extras in Clinton's marketing plan. The Americans have already decided to do everything without us. They see us as crap."[9]

It is unlikely that Blair will become similarly unhappy with Clinton, but one of the unanswered questions about the expansion concerns where leadership will come from. If the U.S. strategic interest in Europe has declined since the end of the Cold War, why should the United States continue to spend so much on ensuring European security? Why not let the Europeans do more for themselves? Such questions are likely to be raised in the United States, and so far Clinton has offered little in the way of answers, aside from the standard rhetoric about the need to encourage democratic (and capitalistic) reforms. The United States may choose to offer such encouragement in a lesser role, while Blair, Chirac, Kohl, and others assume greater leadership responsibilities.

How NATO is to be led cannot be determined until decisions are made about what NATO is to do. The expansion discussions took place with only minimal attention being paid to defining the mission of the new NATO. A crucial question in this matter is what the United States will do. A report prepared by the German parliament in 1997 said, "Bosnia has made clear that effective conflict resolution in Europe is possible at the present time only with the active involvement of the United States."[10] A U.S. withdrawal from Bosnia would certainly result in the immediate departure of other peacekeepers. If the war in the former Yugoslavia then resumed, NATO's ineffectiveness as Europe's police force would be proved, and questions would arise about the purpose of the organization's expansion. To prevent this collapse of NATO's authority, its members—principally, in this case, the United States, Great Britain, and France—will have to muster the political will to take the risks necessary to work through the stubborn problems in the Balkans.

The Bosnia test, as complicated as it may seem, is merely a microcosmic example of what may become the broadened mission of NATO. The task of protecting the member states from external aggression becomes obsolete when there is no external aggressor. But most of these same states have vital security interests elsewhere. Since World War II, the United States has been counted on to take care of these out-of-area problems, most recently by assembling the coalition to fight Iraq in the Persian Gulf War. The United States has no reason to remain in that position indefinitely; the economic, political, and human costs are too high. Europe needs to start taking better care of its own interests.

America and Europe, a thoughtful book published in 1997 under the auspices of RAND Studies in Policy Analysis, proposes a "new strategic bargain" between the United States and its European allies. In simplified form, the U.S. proposal would amount to this: "We'll stay in Europe if you'll help us manage affairs in the rest of the world." The necessity for such a deal is rooted in U.S. domestic politics. Without formalized burden sharing, Congress might not continue funding a sizable U.S. presence in Europe.

The idea makes sense, but so far it appears to have stimulated little response within the Clinton administration. RAND's Ronald Asmus writes: "No serious effort has emerged from the U.S. side to propose, let alone build, a new transatlantic relationship that would strike a new balance between 'keeping Europe stable' and managing shared international security concerns beyond Europe. . . . Indeed, a quick look at U.S. defense planning suggests that Washington does not expect its European allies to play a major role in future contingencies beyond Europe." Asmus notes that although the United States is a member of a formal alliance, NATO, in Europe, it takes an ad hoc approach to problems elsewhere, which means maintaining a costly military capability to deal unilaterally with future conflicts in the Middle East, Northeast Asia, and other places.[11]

The Europeans have long enjoyed this arrangement. By letting the United States do the heavy lifting, they have received protection at minimal cost. As long as the Soviet Union had to be countered around the world, this made some sense, since only the United States could mount a credible response to a Soviet threat. But Iraq, North Korea, and various other troublemakers are not as imposing.

To reassert its friendship with the United States and its leadership in Europe, Great Britain could take the initiative on its side of the Atlantic in crafting the new strategic bargain. NATO members' interests need to be redefined in the context of global realism, not confined by Europe's boundaries. NATO stands as the most powerful alliance in the world, and it should not be disingenuous about its muscle.

Such assumption of broader responsibility also would make NATO expansion less necessary. An expanded mission would certainly include preserving stability in Central and Eastern Europe. This implicit guarantee would be far less provocative toward Russia than would formal incorporation within NATO of nations near or at Russia's borders.

Great Britain's activism in this effort would be the logical next step in the maturation of the special relationship. Prime Minister Blair clearly is one of the ascendant leaders of Europe, and Britain may be the most politically and economically stable European power at the moment. Anglo-American friendship would be fortified if the two countries exercised joint leadership in this venture.

While this grand scheme for NATO's new mission develops, continuation of internal redesign would also be appropriate. Further cooperation between NATO and the Western European Union is probably the most sensible way to enhance a European defense identity that achieves three principal objectives: giving European states a cohesive forum for establishing their own defense policy; ensuring coordination between NATO and the EU, which will be particularly important if both organizations expand; and recognizing that the essential ingredient of NATO, the United States as active participant, must be preserved, no matter what other alterations in the European security structure may take place.

This last objective remains the most important, but one of the realities of the new century will be the need for Europe to become more capable of defending itself. Great Britain has the best military in Europe, although the French might quarrel about that and the Germans may soon reach the same level. Britain therefore should take the lead both in the operations of any European defense organization and in being the bridge between Europe and the United States.

In all defense matters, the role of Germany should be pondered carefully. Perhaps there are limits to the extent to which the past should haunt the future. Nevertheless, extraordinary caution should be exercised before putting Germany in a position in which it feels it must become more militarily assertive.

Behind any debate about security measures should be the realization that the new Europe cannot succeed if it is merely a mildly revised version of what has gone before. Concepts of trust and autonomy must be redefined, and the immeasurable value of a peaceful Europe should always be kept in mind. About this, Vaclav Havel wrote:

> European integration should—and must, if it is to succeed—enable all the nationalities to realize their national autonomy within the framework of a broad civil society created by the supernational community. The greatness of this idea lies in its power to smother the demons of nationalism, those instigators of modern wars, and to enable nations to live in peace, security, freedom, and prosperity by forgoing some of their immediate interests in favor of the far greater benefits of realizing their long-term interests.[12]

While debate about NATO and other security issues has received much attention from British and U.S. leaders and at least some from the public, the economic links between the two countries have attracted less scrutiny. These ties have never been sturdier, and they show every indication of becoming even stronger and better balanced. Investment and trade in both goods and services are being driven by a number of factors: strong economies in both countries; aggressive efforts by both governments to stimulate transatlantic business growth; nongovernmental, business-to-business projects to expand economic activity; and the general comfort level provided by having similar business institutions and practices.

The amount of activity is particularly surprising because it simply goes on steadily with little public attention being paid to it. Most Americans, for example, are probably unaware that Great Britain has supplanted Japan as the number one outside investor in the United States. Similarly, many Britons probably do not know how their own service industries are expanding to meet the demands of U.S. companies wanting their help in doing business both in Great Britain and on the Continent.

The two governments have been generally supportive of trade and investment expansion. The task now involves something governments are not very good at: backing away and letting business take care of itself. The principal role for government now is that of a supporting player, clearing away obstacles to even freer trade. This means coordinating standards and reducing de facto protectionism, such as "Buy American" procurement policies.

One of the most helpful elements in Anglo-American business relations is the almost total absence of xenophobia toward each other. Americans and Britons do not seem very "foreign" to each other, and as a result, there is minimal wariness about the size of investment in each other's country. This is not to say that national loyalties have weakened. Rather, there is a foundation of trust between citizens of the two nations that is grounded in cultural sameness. A less kind way of looking at this is to theorize that white Americans and Britons prefer each other because they harbor race-based or similar discriminatory distrust of Japanese, Arabs, and others who do not share that sameness.

The closeness of business relationships strengthens Anglo-American ties in other matters. In the absence of the international crises that in the past have pulled the countries more tightly together, economic issues may become the driving force behind the Anglo-American relationship. The economic picture is, however, made far more complicated by multilateral concerns that transcend the two countries' business links to one another. The European Union presents distinct challenges to Great Britain and the United States. The British at least are considering the issues involved, such as the potential clout of this mature version of the Common Market and the need to balance sovereignty and cooperation. The American public, however, is largely ignorant about ramifications of the

EU's operations. Few Americans know, for example, that the EU's economy is considerably larger than that of the United States.

Despite the relative cordiality of relations between the United States
and EU members now, transatlantic economic competition will inevitably increase. How that competition takes shape is of utmost importance:

- Will the EU remain committed to free trade, or will it gradually become
  an economic "fortress Europe"?
- Will the United States devise an appropriately sophisticated approach to
  this evolution in the balance of international economic power, or will it
  continue to presume that it is the ultimate "bigfoot," able to dominate
  international economic policy indefinitely?

So far, the EU has shown no significant signs of slipping into protectionism. Its members profess allegiance to free trade and realize that they
will profit most by building bridges to other trading partners. Nevertheless, it is only natural that favoritism develops among club members.

The United States will watch this warily and may look to Great Britain—probably the EU member most committed to free trade—to help
keep channels between the United States and the EU clear of obstruction.
Great Britain will probably be inclined to do this, but for its part must
be careful not to be perceived as being merely a U.S. stalking horse within
EU councils.

During the next few years, the EU may be tempted to flex its muscles
occasionally while it establishes itself as a new, collective superpower.
Possessing that clout is an important motivation for EU members. Former
German chancellor Helmut Schmidt points out that although none of
the EU states individually wields influence comparable to that of what
he considers the three superpowers—the United States, China, and Russia—the EU collectively can do so. "This perception," he says, "is gaining
ground among members of the EU, and it provides an additional strategic
motivation for European integration."[13]

The EU also will be addressing two big internal issues, monetary union
and membership expansion, that will affect the United States but have
yet to be adequately addressed by U.S. policy makers. If the European
Monetary Union works well—and that "if" looms large in the minds of
many—it will greatly enhance the EU's economic power. It will end
drastic currency fluctuations and reduce transaction costs, which should
spur further investment. Also, it will impose, via the independent Euro-

pean Central Bank, much-needed discipline on member states' economies, reining in inflation, interest rates, and debt and otherwise de-
manding that EU nations adhere to the common standards on which
EMU is being built.

Anything that so thoroughly affects Europe's economy will also have
a profound impact on the United States. A stronger Europe would be a
good match with a booming United States, but U.S. business must move
assertively both to expand in Europe and to attract European investment
in the United States. In all such transatlantic activity, Great Britain can
be a key player. It has much to offer and gain itself in trade and investment, and in a gateway role it can assist the transatlantic flow of goods
and money. Much of this is going on already, driven by market forces.
The respective governments do not need to do much except get out of
the way, taking with them as many barriers as possible.

Great Britain's Tony Blair faces a delicate task in leading his country
toward or away from EMU. He is committed to a strong EU economy,
but not necessarily to EMU. During his 1997 campaign, he embraced a
moderate Euroskepticism, avoiding the Tories' hysterics but also making
clear that he would lead Britain slowly and carefully toward any new
monetary arrangement.

Now that Great Britain has decided on a wait-and-see policy about
EMU, Americans will watch carefully. A brief delay would probably affect
U.S. businesses only slightly, but if it appears that Britain is drifting too
far away from the EU mainstream, then some U.S. businesses might decide to bypass Britain as gateway or launching pad and plunge directly
into the EU action. On the other hand, if Britain delays and EMU runs
into problems after its birth, then Britain may seem even more appealing
as a place to do business.

The Blair government and other decision makers in Britain recognize
the conflicting pressures about EMU. Chancellor Gordon Brown said in
July 1997 that "whether Britain is in or out of EMU will have profound
implications for Britain's business and Britain's economy."[14] A July 1997
survey of the Confederation of British Industry found that only 10 percent
of its members wanted to rule out joining EMU forever. The apparent
majority sentiment within this organization, which represents British big
business, is to take a pass on 1999 entry and join later.

One concern for British policy makers is a possible division within the
EU between EMU members and nonmembers. If the monetary union
works well, the first-wave members might start coordinating their economic policies, leaving Great Britain and other late starters on the side-

lines. Although EU treaties and the independent European Central Bank will govern most fiscal and trade matters, two-tier decision making is a possibility that British leaders will watch for.[15]

Concurrent with its EMU efforts, the EU will be expanding. In some ways, this will be more complicated than the similar growth of NATO, even though many of the same players are involved. The three proposed new NATO members, Poland, Hungary, and the Czech Republic, plus Cyprus, Slovenia, and Estonia are the principal candidates to join the EU in 2002. Looking eastward certainly is popular at the moment; members of the Western military and economic alliances seem determined to embrace former foes and outsiders, regardless of the difficulties of engineering such a hug and paying the attendant costs. For example, the six new EU applicants have an average per capita GDP that is only 13 percent of the EU average.

A major sticking point for expansion (and for EU finances generally) is the Common Agricultural Policy (CAP). Created to spur free trade in agricultural products within Europe, CAP paid the same guaranteed prices to all farmers in member states. Farmers took advantage of this, lobbying for higher prices and producing huge surpluses. As a result, almost half the EU budget is devoted to CAP.

The economies of the Eastern European EU applicants are more agriculture oriented than those of current members. If CAP were to go unchanged, the overall EU budget would have to expand by almost 50 percent to cover CAP payments to the new members. But some reforms are under way. CAP farm support prices have been pulled down closer to world levels, bringing some much-needed realism and savings to the CAP budget. Great Britain has endorsed CAP reforms both as a sound general idea and as being essential to keeping the overall EU operating budget limited to no more than 1.27 percent of the EU's overall gross national product (GNP).

From the U.S. standpoint, benefits of EU expansion outweigh the problems it might cause. The principal advantage would be having the EU discipline imposed on the developing economies of Eastern Europe. Left to themselves, the fiscal policies of these countries might lurch wildly, but with the enticement of membership in such a powerful club, these states would be unlikely to stray too far. The resulting economic stability would mean enhanced markets for U.S. trade.

The political dimension of EU expansion is harder to evaluate. As with NATO, "good behavior" concerning democratic process and human rights is a prerequisite for prospective members, although the definition of "good" is vague. The eastward expansion of the EU, therefore, could be hoped to limit political as well as economic volatility. One intriguing prospect involves Turkey, which for more than thirty years has wanted to become a full citizen of Europe's economic community. Although EU officials have criticized Turkey's human rights record, admitting Turkey to the club would be a useful sign to the Muslim world that different cultures need not always clash.

The Clinton administration has quietly encouraged EU expansion not only for economic reasons but also as a means to further political stability. Peace is most likely to endure when economies are strong, and, in turn, prosperity is most likely to flourish when political tensions are minimal. Great Britain also has been supportive. Foreign Secretary Robin Cook said of the initial expansion planning, "Enlargement is a central objective for the U.K. and the E.U." He noted that this planning should encompass reform of CAP and other EU structural matters, reflecting the British position that the EU must change as it grows.[16]

The New Transatlantic Agenda, agreed to by the United States and the EU at the 1995 Madrid summit, established a framework for consultation between U.S. and EU officials and prescribed a range of joint initiatives about security and trade matters. Questions remain about how avidly either side will pursue this relationship, but the door has been opened for continued U.S.-EU cooperation.

EU expansion almost certainly will proceed, perhaps with creation of a subsidiary organization to assist prospective members while they await full membership. If these emerging economies can shape up and meet the EU's standards, Europe will be more stable and prosperous. But the EU must resist the temptation to relax standards to any considerable degree in order to accommodate the candidates. Sliding down to the lowest common denominator might make everyone happy, but only briefly. One of the EU's greatest assets is its structural integrity. Great Britain, as a cautious member, and the United States, as a cautious observer, should exert their influence to make certain that not too high a price is paid for eastward expansion. Robin Cook has said that the EU should be open to all of Europe, telling potential members, "If you are ready, then you can join." The catch, of course, is in being "ready."

Whatever the new configuration of the EU may be, the United States should expect increased competition from across the Atlantic. For the moment, at least, the EU seems to be more dynamic and aggressive than the United States is in making new trade deals, even within the Western Hemisphere.

The goal of some U.S. policy planners is to see NAFTA superseded within a decade by a Free Trade Area of the Americas (FTAA), which would cover all the nations of the hemisphere (except perhaps Cuba, if Castroism still prevails there). Many Latin American economies, such as those of Brazil, Chile, and Argentina, are steadily growing stronger, so the FTAA might prove to be a potent counterpart to the EU.

The Europeans, however, are not sitting back and waiting for this to happen. They are instead making their own deals in Latin America, particularly with the Mercosur countries—Argentina, Brazil, Paraguay, and Uruguay. By 1995, Mercosur trade with the EU totaled $43 billion; with the United States, $29 billion. This has led Chile, impatient with U.S. promises about bringing it into NAFTA, to become an associate member of Mercosur. Within the next few years, Mercosur and the EU may form their own free-trade area.[17]

The United States should certainly not have expected to monopolize a hemisphere's worth of trade, but the assertiveness of the EU effort is nonetheless surprising. It illustrates that those who preach "global free trade," as the United States does, should be prepared to see it happen.

Competition between the United States and the EU will intensify, but it can do so more or less amicably. Great Britain may find itself playing with both sides, being a leading force within the EU while it is still a trusted friend of the United States. That will require some tightrope walking, but it is the kind of task Britain has undertaken before. For the United States, it is extremely important that Britain be willing to play this dual role. Otherwise, the Atlantic might become a barrier to trade and growth.

Another potential transatlantic problem is sluggishness in removing non-tariff barriers to trade. Politicians might be tempted to rally behind a formal Transatlantic Free Trade Agreement (TAFTA) designed principally to eliminate the relatively insignificant tariffs that still exist. This could be accomplished with a great deal of ceremony, but it would have minimal impact. The real way to open trade further is to limit the parochial regulations, product standards, and subsidies that create a de facto protectionism. That can be done quietly and effectively, in many cases industry by industry, with attentive governments taking their cues from the businesses that do the trading. A TAFTA has a certain allure, but it really is not necessary. The case that can be made for it is based more on politics than on economics.

Beyond the politics—the security arrangements, the trade agreements, and other elements of diplomatic partnership—relations between the United States and Great Britain continue to draw their strength from deep-rooted affinities and mutual admiration. In 1876, Ralph Waldo Emerson wrote of Great Britain, "It is the land of patriots, martyrs, sages and bards, and if the ocean out of which it emerged should wash it away, it will be remembered as an island famous for immortal laws, for the announcements of original right which make the stone tables of liberty."[18] That is a classical American view, archaic in its phrasing, but even today consistent with the fundamental U.S. attitude about Britain. Echoes of Emerson's observation could be heard 120 years later in Margaret Thatcher's appraisal of why Anglo-American ties remain so strong:

> The reason our interests have so often coincided is not merely expediency but because we stand upon the same hallowed moral ground: an enduring belief in the sanctity of the individual, a commitment to democracy and representative government, common religious traditions, and an unfaltering dedication to the rule of law. And it has been by our willingness to defend those basic principles that America and Britain have served as a beacon to the world, lighting the way through the darkest days of this century.[19]

Reinforcing these shared ideals is the common language, the foundation for grand and mundane aspects of the relationship. Much tradition grows from the language, and so too does the day-to-day life of the two countries. People doing business, tourists on the prowl, government officials sharing ideas: everything is so much easier because of the English language, particularly when it is coupled with social conventions that are so similar. A layer of tension that is normal in international relations vanishes because of this. (One of the reasons the common language is so important is the notorious inability of most Americans to speak anything other than English.)

This comfort level should not, however, create the impression that U.S. and British national interests converge completely. The nations' roles in the world differ greatly, and not everything that is good for one is good for the other. Recognizing this and avoiding presumptuousness is important. The special character of the relationship has its limits. Great Britain may be more tolerant than other nations are of U.S. behavior that is perceived as haughty, but particularly when Britain has a prime minister as ambitious and assertive as Tony Blair, arrogance in Washington might lead to problems. "Hegemony" is a dirty word in the post–Cold War world, and American leaders should take note of that.

The Clinton administration's foreign policy making often proceeds with a naïveté that is more unsettling than charming. Granted, the challenges Clinton faces are unprecedented; he is the first president to take office with the Cold War truly over and with the Soviet Union gone. As leader of what is clearly the sole superpower, at least for the moment, Clinton sometimes faces the temptation to charge up the hill while assuming that others will follow.

That style of leadership will almost certainly breed resentment among the putative followers, as was the case when the United States in 1997 dictated the specifics of NATO's expansion. This rankled particularly because the United States had been seen by some of those same "followers" as lagging behind them several years earlier when intervention was needed in the former Yugoslavia. Even a most stalwart friend, such as Great Britain, will occasionally be irritated by the apparent thirst of the United States for leadership without responsibility.

U.S. rhetoric about such matters remains high-flown but often vague. In June 1997, Secretary of State Madeleine Albright described alternative paths the United States could take:

> A decade or two from now, we will be known as the neo-isolationists, who allowed tyranny and lawlessness to rise again, or as the generations that solidified the global triumph of democratic principles. We will be known as the neo-protectionists, whose lack of vision produced financial meltdown, or as the generations that laid the groundwork for rising prosperity around the world. We will be known as the world-class ditherers, who stood by while the seeds of renewed global conflict were sown, or as the generations that took strong measures to forge alliances, deter aggression, and keep the peace.[20]

Although the preferences among these options are clear, the path the United States and its allies might take to get from here to there remains undiscovered. It is unlikely to appear magically on its own; the challenge of leadership is to find it, broaden it, and improve it.

On a more purely bilateral level as well, the United States should be careful about lapsing into carelessness. For instance, the Clinton administration only belatedly recognized that a certain deference to British sensitivities should accompany U.S. efforts to help end the conflict in Northern Ireland. What appeared in Washington to be noble statesmanship was seen in London as condescension and meddling. Even after two centuries, handling of the Anglo-American relationship sometimes lacks common sense. All parties should realize that the reservoir of good will between the United States and Great Britain is deep but not bottomless.

It is also important that in U.S. eyes Great Britain's identity remain distinguishable from that of the collective Europe. The theory of a federalized Europe is worrisome to many Britons because it implies loss of sovereignty at numerous levels. But as a practical matter, any such federalism is likely to operate within relatively narrow limits. There are too many historical sensitivities and too much loyalty to national traditions for the lines between states to become overly blurred. Nevertheless, there may be a tendency for an outsider, such as the United States, to adopt a simplistic view of Europe, particularly as the EU becomes better established. This would be a serious mistake. "Europe" will never be as reliable a friend for the United States as Great Britain is.

Despite the importance of not letting itself be subsumed by Europe, Great Britain must remain a leading player in NATO, the EU, and European affairs generally, or else the United States might turn away from Britain in favor of building a closer relationship with others (Germany being the most likely candidate) who can do more to advance the European interests of the United States. What Britons consider to be their prudence about EMU could come to be seen by the United States as a failure of nerve that relegates Britain to a second tier of allies.

Although the British must do what they think best for themselves about the common currency, they should understand that as far as U.S. policy makers are concerned, their actions will have consequences. The United States, for its part, should appreciate the complex uncertainties that Great Britain and other European nations face during this period of political and economic transition. Some forbearance on the part of U.S. leaders would be wise; let the dust settle before making decisions that may alter important relationships.

The EMU debate, like the choices about NATO's future, may foreshadow much that lies ahead for the Anglo-American partnership. Great Britain is a principal in European change, while the United States is something slightly less: closely tied to Europe but not part of it; a de facto European power but also an outsider.

Much of the future of Anglo-American relations will be shaped within the context of the two countries' larger world roles, but the essence of the partnership will continue to be grounded in the close ties that have existed for more than 200 years and that have done so much to determine the state of the world as it moves into the next century. True friendship, whether between people or nations, is a treasure that never comes easily, is never serene, and can evaporate quickly. It should be cherished and nurtured when it is found. With this in mind, the United States and Great Britain ought to acknowledge anew how important their relationship is and take all needed steps to ensure that it will endure.

In *Hamlet*, Polonius tells Laertes, "Those friends thou hast, and their adoption tried, / Grapple them to thy soul with hoops of steel." Good advice.

NOTES

CHAPTER ONE—"THE SPECIAL RELATIONSHIP"

1. David Cannadine (ed.), *Blood, Toil, Tears, and Sweat: The Speeches of Winston Churchill* (Boston: Houghton Mifflin, 1989), 301, 308.

2. Benjamin Woods Labaree, *The Boston Tea Party* (Boston: Northeastern University Press, 1979), 141.

3. Peter D. G. Thomas, *Tea Party to Independence* (Oxford: Oxford University Press, 1991), 21.

4. Jack M. Sosin, *Agents and Merchants* (Lincoln: University of Nebraska Press, 1965), 168.

5. W. B. Allen (ed.), *George Washington: A Collection* (Indianapolis: LibertyClassics, 1988), 36.

6. Don Cook, *The Long Fuse: How England Lost the American Colonies, 1760–1785* (New York: Atlantic Monthly Press, 1995), 124.

7. David Hackett Fischer, *Paul Revere's Ride* (New York: Oxford University Press, 1994), 321.

8. G. R. Gleig, *The Campaigns of the British Army at Washington and New Orleans* (Totowa, NJ: Rowman and Littlefield, 1972), 70.

9. James Morton Smith (ed.), *The Republic of Letters* (New York: Norton, 1995), 1744.

10. Norman MacKenzie and Jeanne MacKenzie, *Dickens: A Life* (New York: Oxford University Press, 1979), 117.

11. Frederick W. Dupee (ed.), *The Selected Letters of Charles Dickens* (New York: Farrar, Straus, and Cudahy, 1960), 57.

12. Charles Dickens, *American Notes* (Oxford: Oxford University Press, 1978), 230, 233.

13. James M. McPherson, *Battle Cry of Freedom* (New York: Oxford University Press, 1988), 311.

14. Henry Adams, *The Education of Henry Adams* (Boston: Houghton Mifflin, 1974), 115.

15. McPherson, *Battle Cry of Freedom*, 587, 664.

16. H. G. Nicholas, *The United States and Britain* (Chicago: University of Chicago Press, 1975), 42.

17. Dickens, *American Notes*, 253.

18. Henry James, *Richard Olney and His Public Service* (Boston: Houghton Mifflin, 1923), 109.

19. Ibid., 116.

20. Ibid., 120.

21. Bradford Perkins, *The Great Rapprochement* (New York: Atheneum, 1968), 15.

22. Forrest Davis, *The Atlantic System* (New York: Reynal and Hitchcock, 1941), 51.

23. H. C. Allen, *Great Britain and the United States* (New York: St. Martin's, 1955), 538.

24. Leon Edel, *Henry James: A Life* (New York: Harper and Row, 1985), 449.

25. H. C. Allen, *Great Britain and the United States*, 539.

26. Arthur S. Link (ed.), *The Papers of Woodrow Wilson*, vol. 53 (Princeton: Princeton University Press, 1986), 550.

27. Ibid., 532, 533.

28. Alan P. Dobson, *Anglo-American Relations in the Twentieth Century* (London: Routledge, 1995), 34.

29. Link, *Papers of Woodrow Wilson*, vol. 53, 558, 563.

30. Ibid., 564.

31. Ibid., 565.

32. Edward R. Murrow, *In Search of Light* (New York: Knopf, 1967), 33.

33. Ibid., 47.

34. Robin Renwick, *Fighting with Allies* (New York: Times Books, 1996), 25.

35. Murrow, *In Search of Light*, 42.

36. H. V. Morton, *Atlantic Meeting* (New York: Dodd, Mead, 1943), 183.

37. Ibid., 185.

38. Ibid., 186.

39. Winston S. Churchill, *Memoirs of the Second World War* (Boston: Houghton Mifflin, 1959), 492.

40. Cannadine, *Blood, Toil, Tears, and Sweat*, 254.

41. Robert Dallek, *Franklin D. Roosevelt and American Foreign Policy, 1932–1945* (New York: Oxford University Press, 1979), 285.

42. Ibid., 288.

43. Ibid., 285.

44. Ibid., 331.

45. Cannadine, *Blood, Toil, Tears, and Sweat*, 230.

46. Ibid., 252, 256.

47. Renwick, *Fighting with Allies*, 220.

48. Peter Grose, *Gentleman Spy: The Life of Allen Dulles* (Boston: Houghton Mifflin, 1994), 433.

49. Donald Neff, *Warriors at Suez* (New York: Linden Press/Simon and Schuster, 1981), 410.

50. Dobson, *Anglo-American Relations*, 118.

51. Neff, *Warriors at Suez*, 291.

52. George F. Kennan, *Memoirs, 1950–1963* (Boston: Atlantic–Little, Brown, 1972), 184.

53. Renwick, *Fighting with Allies*, 227.

54. Henry Kissinger, *Diplomacy* (New York: Simon and Schuster, 1994), 598.

55. John Dickie, *"Special" No More* (London: Weidenfeld and Nicolson, 1994), 175.

56. Renwick, *Fighting with Allies*, 341.

57. Nicholas Henderson, *Channels and Tunnels* (London: Weidenfeld and Nicolson, 1987), 101.

58. Dickie, *"Special" No More*, 3–6.

59. Henderson, *Channels and Tunnels*, 108.

60. Geoffrey Smith, *Reagan and Thatcher* (New York: Norton, 1991), 125.

61. Margaret Thatcher, *The Downing Street Years* (New York: HarperCollins, 1993), 331.

62. George P. Shultz, *Turmoil and Triumph* (New York: Scribner's, 1993), 340.

63. Thatcher, *Downing Street Years*, 334.

64. Renwick, *Fighting with Allies*, 360.

65. Ibid., 361.

66. Thatcher, *Downing Street Years*, 444.

67. Ibid., 783.

68. Tony Blair, *New Britain* (London: Fourth Estate, 1996), 210.

69. Ibid., 266–267.

70. Bill Clinton, speech to the Houses of Parliament, London, November 29, 1995, 3.

71. "Global Responses to Global Challenges," press conference of Prime Minister Tony Blair and President Bill Clinton, London, May 29, 1997, 1.

72. Ibid.

73. Quoted by Malcolm Rifkind, "Principles and Practices of British Foreign Policy," speech at Chatham House, London, September 21, 1995.

CHAPTER TWO—DEFENDERS OF THE FAITH

1. Margaret Thatcher, *The Path to Power* (New York: HarperCollins, 1995), 512.

2. John E. Rielly (ed.), *American Public Opinion and U.S. Foreign Policy, 1995* (Chicago: Chicago Council on Foreign Relations, 1995), 23, 25.

3. "Public Indifferent about NATO Expansion," news release, Pew Research Center for the People and the Press, January 24, 1997, 2.

4. Robert C. Toth, *America's Place in the World, II* (Washington, DC: Pew Research Center for the People and the Press, 1997), 1, 15.

5. Kissinger, *Diplomacy*, 819, 821.

6. Author interview with Raymond Seitz, April 23, 1997.

7. John Kerr, untitled speech about U.S.-British relations, San Diego, California, December 13, 1996.

8. Michael Stürmer, "Germany in Search of an Enlightened American Leadership," in *In Search of a New World Order*, ed. Henry Brandon (Washington, DC: Brookings Institution, 1992), 80.

9. Author interview with Michael Mandelbaum, March 3, 1997.

10. Beatrice Heuser, *Transatlantic Relations* (London: Pinter/Royal Institute of International Affairs, 1996), 91.

11. Samuel P. Huntington, *The Clash of Civilizations and the Remaking of World Order* (New York: Simon and Schuster, 1996), 161.

12. Aleksei K. Pushkov, "The Risk of Losing Russia," *New York Times*, January 21, 1997, A19.

13. John Major, speech about European security to WEU Parliamentary Assembly, London, February 23, 1996, cited in *Survey of Current Affairs*, March 1996, 87.

14. Richard H. Ullman, *Securing Europe* (Princeton: Princeton University Press, 1991), 65.

15. Ronald D. Asmus, "Double Enlargement: Redefining the Atlantic Partnership after the Cold War," in *America and Europe*, ed. David C. Gompert and F. Stephen Larrabee (New York: Cambridge University Press, 1997), 41.

16. Ibid., 23.

17. Thatcher, *Path to Power*, 533.

18. James A. Thomson, "A New Partnership, New NATO Military Structures," in *America and Europe*, ed. Gompert and Larrabee, 80, 90.

19. Author interview with Dick Cheney, August 6, 1997.

20. Author interview with Laurence Martin, April 8, 1997.

21. Author interview with Douglas Hurd, April 7, 1997.

22. Author interview with Dick Cheney, August 6, 1997.

23. Laurence Martin, "Risky Rush for a Doubtful Goal," *The World Today*, February 1997, 51.

24. Author interview with Douglas Hurd, April 7, 1997.

25. Author interview with Raymond Seitz, April 23, 1997.

26. Robin Cook, "British Foreign Policy: Mission Statement," press conference, London, May 12, 1997.

27. Author interview with Raymond Seitz, April 23, 1997.

28. Tad Szulc, "A Looming Greek Tragedy in Hong Kong," *Foreign Policy*, no. 106, Spring 1997, 78.

29. Christopher Lockwood, "China Exposes the EU's Lack of Diplomacy," *Daily Telegraph*, April 21, 1997, 12.

30. "Global Responses to Global Challenges," press conference of Prime Minister Tony Blair and President Bill Clinton, London, May 29, 1997, 3.

31. Author interview with Douglas Hurd, April 7, 1997.

32. Denis Healey, *The Time of My Life* (New York: Norton, 1989), 528.

33. Thatcher, *Downing Street Years*, 568.

34. James Chace, *The Consequences of the Peace* (New York: Twentieth Century Fund/Oxford University Press, 1992), 79.

35. "The Future of Warfare," *The Economist*, March 8, 1997, 15.

36. "New Labour's Model Army," *The Economist*, September 27, 1997, 62.

37. Author interview with Dick Cheney, August 6, 1997.

38. Renwick, *Fighting with Allies*, 403.

39. Ibid., 402.

40. Christopher Andrew, *Her Majesty's Secret Service* (New York: Penguin, 1987), 492.

41. Author interview with Dick Cheney, August 6, 1997.

42. Author interview with William Crowe, April 24, 1997.

43. William Wallace, "On the Move—Destination Unknown," *The World Today*, April 1997, 101.

44. Heuser, *Transatlantic Relations*, 95.

45. William J. Crowe, Jr., "Transatlantic Relations and the Future of European Security," speech to the Royal Institute of International Affairs, London, October 25, 1996, 6.

46. Author interview with Dick Cheney, August 6, 1997.

47. Author interview with Charles Powell, April 22, 1997.

48. Robin Cook, "European Security and Defense," press conference at the WEU Ministerial Meeting, Paris, May 13, 1997.

49. Tony Blair, "Amsterdam Summit," statement to the House of Commons, June 18, 1997.

50. Heuser, *Transatlantic Relations*, 71.

51. Roland Smith, "A Changing NATO," *NATO Review*, May-June 1997, 10.

52. Heuser, *Transatlantic Relations*, 97.

53. Rifkind, "Principles and Practices of British Foreign Policy."

54. Huntington, *Clash of Civilizations*, 21, 258.

55. Michael Mandelbaum, *The Dawn of Peace in Europe* (New York: Twentieth Century Fund, 1996), 159.

56. Renwick, *Fighting with Allies*, 405.

57. Heuser, *Transatlantic Relations*, 73.

58. John Van Oudenaren, "Europe as Partner," in *America and Europe*, ed. Gompert and Larrabee, 125.

CHAPTER THREE—DOLLARS AND POUNDS

1. Author interview with Douglas Hurd, April 7, 1997.

2. Kenneth Clarke, "Britain and the U.S.," speech to the Pilgrims Dinner, London, February 15, 1995.

3. Author interview with Alistair Hunter, April 7, 1997.

4. "Focus on Britain," Foreign and Commonwealth Office, March 1996, 14.

5. "One Hundred Facts on London," London First Centre, June 1996, 16–17.

6. "Invest in Britain Bureau Review of Operations, 1996," Department of Trade and Industry, 1996, 14.

7. Ibid., 4.

8. Steve Lohr, "Microsoft Picks England as Site of Research Lab," *New York Times*, June 18, 1997, C1.

9. Author interview with Andrew Fraser, April 23, 1997.

10. Clarke, "Britain and the U.S."

11. Author interview with Sandy Gardiner, April 7, 1997.

12. Author interview with Charles Ford, April 9, 1997.

13. Jeffrey E. Garten, "America, Europe, and Germany: Commercial Relations for a New Era," speech to the American Institute for Contemporary German Studies, New York, October 17, 1994, 19.

14. Author interview with Andrew Fraser, April 23, 1997.

15. Malcolm Rifkind, "The Transatlantic Partnership: The Future Economic Agenda," speech to the Transatlantic Policy Network, London, February 6, 1996.

16. Ibid.

17. Roberts, Roach, & Associates, "Economic Benefits of U.S.-U.K. Open Skies," study prepared for American Airlines, Inc., October 1996.

18. Stanley Reed, "A Jolly Good Deal for Merrill Lynch," *Business Week*, December 1, 1997, 154.

19. "Commercial Service—London: An Overview," United States Embassy, London, March 1997, 2.

20. British Tourist Authority, "National Facts of Tourism," October 1996.

21. James Schlesinger, "An American Assessment: 'Hands across the Sea' Less Firmly Clasped," in *In Search of a New World Order*, ed. Brandon, 150.

22. Rifkind, "Transatlantic Partnership."

23. Blair, *New Britain*, 267.

24. Stephen Woolcock, *Market Access Issues in EC-US Relations* (London: Pinter/Royal Institute of International Affairs, 1991), 7.

25. Malcolm Rifkind, "Transatlantic Free Trade," speech to the British-American Business Council, London, March 12, 1996.

26. David C. Gompert, "America as Partner," in *America and Europe*, ed. Gompert and Larrabee, 161.

27. Author interview with Douglas Hurd, April 7, 1997.

28. Larry Rohter, "Trade Storm Imperils Caribbean Banana Crops," *New York Times*, May 9, 1997, A6.

29. Blair, *New Britain*, 283.

30. Author interview with Alistair Hunter, April 7, 1997.

31. "Britain's Overseas Trade," Foreign and Commonwealth Office, March 1994.

32. Henry Brandon, "A More Promising Era Beckons at Last," in *In Search of a New World Order*, ed. Brandon, 161.

33. "Ready or Not, Here Comes EMU," *The Economist*, October 11, 1997, 22.

34. Jacques Santer, "Britain's Rightful Place," *The Economist*, May 10, 1997, 50.

35. Martin Kettle, "Background to the Debate," in *The Single Currency: Should Britain Join?* by Martin Kettle, John Palmer, Larry Elliott, and Victor Keegan (London: Vintage, 1997), 13.

36. Gordon Brown, "European and Economic Union," statement to the House of Commons, October 27, 1997, 6.

37. Rudi Dornbusch, "Monetary Union Might Just Put the Spring Back in Europe's Step," *Business Week*, December 23, 1996, 24.

38. Tony Judt, "Continental Rift," *New York Times*, June 5, 1997, A21.

39. Leonhard Gleske, "The Opportunities and Perils for the United States of European Integration," in *In Search of a New World Order*, ed. Brandon, 105.

40. C. Fred Bergsten, "The Dollar and the Euro," *Foreign Affairs* 76, no. 4, July/August 1997, 84.

41. Clarke, "Britain and the U.S."

42. Blair, *New Britain*, 210.

43. Author interview with Nicholas Henderson, April 7, 1997.

44. Author interview with Douglas Hurd, April 7, 1997.

45. Author interview with Alistair Hunter, April 7, 1997.

46. Heuser, *Transatlantic Relations*, 82.

47. Thatcher, *Path to Power*, 622.

48. Rifkind, "Transatlantic Partnership."

49. Author interview with Charles Powell, April 22, 1997.

50. Ian Lang, "Europe and America—Natural Partners," speech to the European Institute, Washington, DC, November 8, 1995.

51. Douglas Hurd, "The Transatlantic Partnership," speech to the Economic

Club, the Chicago Council on Foreign Relations, and the Union League Club, Chicago, May 18, 1995.

52. Blair, *New Britain*, 267.

53. Van Oudenaren, "Europe as Partner," 135.

54. Author interview with Raymond Seitz, April 23, 1997.

55. Woolcock, *Market Access Issues*, 93.

56. "Global Defence Industry Survey," *The Economist*, June 14, 1997, 17.

57. Hurd, "Transatlantic Partnership."

58. Rifkind, "Transatlantic Partnership."

59. Woolcock, *Market Access Issues*, 72.

60. Ibid., 81.

61. Andrew Kohut and Robert C. Toth, "Trade and the Public," news release, Times Mirror Center for the People and the Press, December 13, 1994.

62. Heuser, *Transatlantic Relations*, 85.

63. Author interview with Alistair Hunter, April 7, 1997.

64. Andrew Kohut and Robert C. Toth, "Public Opinion and Trade Policy," news release, Times Mirror Center for the People and the Press, December 15, 1995.

65. Paulo Wrobel, "Towards a Beautiful Horizon?" *The World Today*, May 1997, 135.

66. Calvin Sims, "Free-Trade Zone of the Americas Given a Go-Ahead," *New York Times*, April 20, 1998, A1.

CHAPTER FOUR—BEYOND *MASTERPIECE THEATRE*

1. Frances Trollope, *Domestic Manners of the Americans* (London: Folio Society, 1974), 242, 56, 91, 50, 123, 87, 169.

2. Anthony Trollope, *Autobiography* (Oxford: Oxford University Press, 1992), 314.

3. Richard Pells, *Not like Us* (New York: Basic Books, 1997), 160.

4. Raymond Seitz, speech to the Pilgrims Society, London, April 19, 1994, 10.

5. Ralph Waldo Emerson, *English Traits* (Boston: Houghton, Mifflin, 1903), 378.

6. Pells, *Not like Us*, 268.

7. Stephen Spender, *Love-Hate Relations* (New York: Random House, 1974), 305.

8. Author interview with David Parker, April 9, 1997.

9. Ibid.

10. Malcolm Bradbury, *Dangerous Pilgrimages* (New York: Viking, 1996), 102.

11. Henry Grunwald, "Jane Austen's Civil Society," *Wall Street Journal*, October 2, 1996, 20.

12. Nigel Nicolson, "Jane Austen's Houses in Fact and Fiction," *Persuasions*, no. 14, 1992, 89.

13. Adam Gopnik, "The Culture of Blairism," *The New Yorker*, July 7, 1997, 30.

14. Alison Boshoff, "Baywatch Cues More Babes," *Daily Telegraph*, April 15, 1997, 12.

15. Author interview with David Evans, British Council, March 4, 1997.

16. "New Focus for the British Movie Industry," *Briefing on Britain* 1, no. 9, 1996, 12.

17. Thomas K. Grose, "Britain Rocks (Not Stonehenge)," *U.S. News and World Report*, March 3, 1997, 13.

18. Alina Tugend, "A British Boom in American Studies," *Chronicle of Higher Education*, April 14, 1995, A40.

19. Pells, *Not like Us*, 124.

20. Author interview with Gary McDowell, April 11, 1997.

21. Ibid.

22. Author interview with David Evans, March 4, 1997.

23. Thomas Jefferson, *Writings* (New York: Library of America, 1984), 1228.

24. Henry Louis Gates, Jr., "Black London," *New Yorker*, April 28, 1997, 199.

25. Warren Hoge, "Tory Leader Asks Delegates to Back a Conservatism That Cares," *New York Times*, October 11, 1997, A2.

26. Jenny Church (ed.), *Social Trends 27* (London: Stationery Office, 1997), 31.

27. Ibid., 30.

28. Kathleen Paul, *Whitewashing Britain* (Ithaca, NY: Cornell University Press, 1997), 190.

29. Pells, *Not like Us*, 309.

CHAPTER FIVE—GETTING ALONG

1. Seitz, speech to the Pilgrims Society, 6.

2. Geoffrey Smith, *Reagan and Thatcher*, 198.

3. Thatcher, *Downing Street Years*, 58.

4. Ibid., 415.

5. Dickie, *"Special" No More*, 199.

6. Geoffrey Smith, *Reagan and Thatcher*, 199.

7. Ibid.

8. Ibid., 201.

9. Ibid.

10. Dickie, *"Special" No More*, 199.

11. James F. Clarity, "Protestants in Ulster Rebuke U.S.," *New York Times*, September 11, 1997, A6.

12. David Sapsted, "Britain Guilty of Genocide, Says Governor," *Daily Telegraph*, October 17, 1996, 20.

13. Conor O'Clery, *The Greening of the White House* (Dublin: Gill and Macmillan, 1996), 23.

14. Martin Walker, *The President We Deserve* (New York: Crown, 1996), 279.

15. O'Clery, *Greening of the White House*, 95.

16. Ibid., 101.

17. Ibid., 119.

18. Walker, *President We Deserve*, 279.

19. Ibid., 280.

20. Bill Clinton, speech to the citizens of Londonderry, Northern Ireland, November 30, 1995.

21. Bill Clinton, speech to the Irish Parliament, Dublin, December 1, 1995.

22. James F. Clarity, "Clinton's Role for Northern Ireland Talks: Restoring the Focus on the Big Picture," *New York Times*, December 5, 1995, A6.

23. Jonathan Stevenson, "Northern Ireland: Treating Terrorists as Statesmen," *Foreign Policy*, no. 105, Winter 1996–97, 129.

24. Author interview with Douglas Hurd, April 7, 1997.

25. Tony Blair, "Northern Ireland," speech to the Royal Ulster Agricultural Show, May 16, 1997.

26. Author interview with Charles Powell, April 22, 1997.

27. Author interview with William Crowe, April 24, 1997.

28. Dickie, *"Special" No More*, 184.

29. Ibid., 185.

30. Thatcher, *Downing Street Years*, 255.

31. Ibid., 256.

32. "UK Will Take All Appropriate Steps to Protect Its Trading Interests (Helms-Burton Legislation)," British Information Services press release, May 3, 1996.

33. Ibid.

34. Walker, *President We Deserve*, 154.

35. Ibid., 155.

36. Peter Goldman, Thomas M. DeFrank, Mark Miller, Andrew Murr, and Tom Mathews, *Quest for the Presidency, 1992* (College Station: Texas A&M University Press, 1994), 518.

37. Walker, *President We Deserve*, 153.

38. O'Clery, *Greening of the White House*, 27.

39. John Rentoul, *Tony Blair* (London: Little, Brown, 1995), 280.

40. "The American Connection," *The Economist*, November 8, 1997, 63.

41. Vaclav Havel, *The Art of the Impossible* (New York: Knopf, 1997), 24.

42. Helmut Schmidt, "Miles to Go," *Foreign Affairs* 76, no. 3, May/June 1997, 219.

43. Henry Kissinger, *White House Years* (Boston: Little, Brown, 1979), 97.

44. Tony Judt, *A Grand Illusion?* (New York: Hill and Wang, 1996), 89.

45. Thatcher, *Downing Street Years*, 789.

46. Ibid., 783.

47. Thatcher, *Path to Power*, 519.

48. Volker Ruhe, "New NATO, New Bundeswehr, and Peace in Bosnia and Herzegovina," *NATO Review*, May–June 1997, 6.

49. H. Schmidt, "Miles to Go," 220.

50. Malcolm Rifkind, "Europe: Which Way Forward?" speech to the Konrad Adenauer Stiftung, Bonn, February 19, 1997.

51. "Germany's Eastward Urge," *The Economist*, March 15, 1997, 49.

52. Blair, *New Britain*, 266.

53. Judt, *Grand Illusion?* 87.

54. Thatcher, *Downing Street Years*, 815.

55. Henderson, *Channels and Tunnels*, 75.

56. John Newhouse, *De Gaulle and the Anglo-Saxons* (New York: Viking, 1970), 351.

57. Henderson, *Channels and Tunnels*, 74.

58. Ibid., 72.

59. Thatcher, *Downing Street Years*, 753.

60. "The Future of Europe," *British Public Opinion*, December 1996, 5.

61. Rielly, *American Public Opinion and U.S. Foreign Policy, 1995*, 22.

62. Henderson, *Channels and Tunnels*, 72.

63. Heuser, *Transatlantic Relations*, 38.

64. Ibid., 35.

65. Ibid., 41.

66. Ibid., 36.

67. Gustav Schmidt, "Historical Traditions and the Inevitability of European Ties," *Annals of the American Academy of Political and Social Science* 538, March 1995, 87.

68. Ibid.

69. Gregory P. Marchildon, "From Pax Britannica to Pax Americana and Beyond," *Annals of the American Academy of Political and Social Science* 538, March 1995, 153.

70. Heuser, *Transatlantic Relations*, 36.

71. Marchildon, "From Pax Britannica," 166, 168.

72. Ibid., 164.

73. Ibid., 159.

74. Ibid., 164.

CHAPTER SIX—THE NEW CENTURY

1. George Gallup, Jr., *The Gallup Poll: Public Opinion, 1994* (Wilmington, DE: Scholarly Resources, 1995), 93.

2. "Attitudes to the Falkland Islands," *British Public Opinion*, September 1995, 6.

3. "The Future of Europe," 5.

4. Rielly, *American Public Opinion and U.S. Foreign Policy, 1995*, 20.

5. Author interview with Robert Worcester, April 15, 1997.

6. Seitz, speech to the Pilgrims Society, 2.

7. Hurd, "Transatlantic Partnership."

8. Author interview with Douglas Hurd, April 7, 1997.

9. William Drozdiak, "How Not to Win Friends and Influence Europe," *Washington Post National Weekly Edition*, July 7, 1997, 18.

10. Craig R. Whitney, "Civil Strife Has NATO Facing Demons Within," *New York Times*, July 6, 1997, 4.

11. Asmus, "Double Enlargement," 47.

12. Havel, *Art of the Impossible*, 130.

13. H. Schmidt, "Miles to Go," 219.

14. "Euro-philia," *The Economist*, July 19, 1997, 50.

15. "Euro-apartheid?" *The Economist*, November 22, 1997, 55.

16. Robin Cook, "European Commission 'Agenda 2000' Communication," statement issued July 16, 1997.

17. Ian Katz, "Is Europe Elbowing the U.S. out of South America?" *Business Week*, August 4, 1997, 56.

18. Emerson, *English Traits*, 308.

19. Margaret Thatcher, "Reason and Religion: The Moral Foundations of Freedom," James Bryce Lecture on the American Commonwealth, Institute of United States Studies, University of London, 1996, 14.

20. Madeleine K. Albright, "Harvard University Commencement Address," *New York Times*, June 6, 1997, A8.

BIBLIOGRAPHY

BOOKS

Adams, Henry. *The Education of Henry Adams*. Boston: Houghton Mifflin, 1974.

Allen, H. C. *Great Britain and the United States*. New York: St. Martin's, 1955.

Allen, W. B. (ed.). *George Washington: A Collection*. Indianapolis: LibertyClassics, 1988.

Andrew, Christopher. *Her Majesty's Secret Service*. New York: Penguin, 1987.

Baker, James A., III. *The Politics of Diplomacy*. New York: Putnam, 1995.

Bartlett, C. J. *"The Special Relationship."* London: Longman, 1992.

Blair, Tony. *New Britain*. London: Fourth Estate, 1996.

Blum, John Morton. *Woodrow Wilson and the Politics of Morality*. Boston: Little, Brown, 1956.

Bradbury, Malcolm. *Dangerous Pilgrimages*. New York: Viking, 1996.

Brandon, Henry (ed.). *In Search of a New World Order*. Washington, DC: Brookings Institution, 1992.

Burke, Edmund. *Speech on Conciliation with America*. Boston: Ginn, 1897.

Cannadine, David (ed.). *Blood, Toil, Tears, and Sweat: The Speeches of Winston Churchill*. Boston: Houghton Mifflin, 1989.

Chace, James. *The Consequences of the Peace*. New York: Twentieth Century Fund/Oxford University Press, 1992.

Church, Jenny (ed.). *Social Trends 27*. London: Stationery Office, 1997.

Churchill, Winston S. *Memoirs of the Second World War*. Boston: Houghton Mifflin, 1959.

Clarke, Michael. *British External Policy-making in the 1990s*. Washington, DC: Brookings Institution/Royal Institute of International Affairs, 1992.

Cloud, Stanley, and Lynne Olson. *The Murrow Boys*. Boston: Houghton Mifflin, 1996.

Cook, Chris, and John Stevenson. *Britain since 1945*. New York: Longman, 1996.

Cook, Don. *The Long Fuse: How England Lost the American Colonies, 1760–1785*. New York: Atlantic Monthly Press, 1995.

Dallek, Robert. *Franklin D. Roosevelt and American Foreign Policy, 1932–1945*. New York: Oxford University Press, 1979.

Davis, Forrest. *The Atlantic System*. New York: Reynal and Hitchcock, 1941.

Dickens, Charles. *American Notes*. Oxford: Oxford University Press, 1978.

Dickie, John. *"Special" No More*. London: Weidenfeld and Nicolson, 1994.

Dobie, J. Frank. *A Texan in England*. Boston: Little, Brown, 1945.

Dobson, Alan P. *Anglo-American Relations in the Twentieth Century*. London: Routledge, 1995.

Dupee, Frederick W. (ed.). *The Selected Letters of Charles Dickens*. New York: Farrar, Straus, and Cudahy, 1960.

Edel, Leon. *Henry James: A Life*. New York: Harper and Row, 1985.

Emerson, Ralph Waldo. *English Traits*. Boston: Houghton, Mifflin, 1903.

Fischer, David Hackett. *Paul Revere's Ride*. New York: Oxford University Press, 1994.

Flexner, James Thomas. *Washington: The Indispensable Man*. Boston: Little, Brown, 1974.

Gallup, George, Jr. *The Gallup Poll: Public Opinion, 1994*. Wilmington, DE: Scholarly Resources, 1995.

Gleig, G. R. *The Campaigns of the British Army at Washington and New Orleans*. Totowa, NJ: Rowman and Littlefield, 1972.

Goldman, Peter, Thomas M. DeFrank, Mark Miller, Andrew Murr, and Tom Mathews. *Quest for the Presidency, 1992*. College Station: Texas A&M University Press, 1994.

Gompert, David C., and F. Stephen Larrabee (eds.). *America and Europe*. New York: Cambridge University Press, 1997.

Goodwin, Doris Kearns. *No Ordinary Time*. New York: Simon and Schuster, 1994.

Grose, Peter. *Gentleman Spy: The Life of Allen Dulles*. Boston: Houghton Mifflin, 1994.

Hathaway, Robert M. *Great Britain and the United States*. Boston: Twayne, 1990.

Havel, Vaclav. *The Art of the Impossible*. New York: Knopf, 1997.

Healey, Denis. *The Time of My Life*. New York: Norton, 1989.

Henderson, Nicholas. *Channels and Tunnels*. London: Weidenfeld and Nicolson, 1987.

Heuser, Beatrice. *Transatlantic Relations*. London: Pinter/Royal Institute of International Affairs, 1996.

Hoopes, Townsend. *The Devil and John Foster Dulles*. Boston: Atlantic–Little, Brown, 1973.

Huntington, Samuel P. *The Clash of Civilizations and the Remaking of World Order*. New York: Simon and Schuster, 1996.

James, Henry. *Richard Olney and His Public Service*. Boston: Houghton Mifflin, 1923.

Jefferson, Thomas. *Writings*. New York: Library of America, 1984.

Judt, Tony. *A Grand Illusion?* New York: Hill and Wang, 1996.

Kennan, George F. *At a Century's Ending*. New York: Norton, 1996.

———. *Memoirs, 1950–1963*. Boston: Atlantic–Little, Brown, 1972.

Kettle, Martin, John Palmer, Larry Elliott, and Victor Keegan. *The Single Currency: Should Britain Join?* London: Vintage, 1997.

Kissinger, Henry. *Diplomacy*. New York: Simon and Schuster, 1994.

———. *White House Years*. Boston: Little, Brown, 1979.

Knock, Thomas J. *To End All Wars*. New York: Oxford University Press, 1992.

Labaree, Benjamin Woods. *The Boston Tea Party*. Boston: Northeastern University Press, 1979.

Link, Arthur S. (ed.). *The Papers of Woodrow Wilson*. Vol. 53. Princeton: Princeton University Press, 1986.

———. *Wilson the Diplomatist*. Chicago: Quadrangle, 1963.

Louis, Wm. Roger, and Hedley Bull (eds.). *The Special Relationship*. Oxford: Oxford University Press, 1986.

MacKenzie, Norman, and Jeanne MacKenzie. *Dickens: A Life*. New York: Oxford University Press, 1979.

Mandelbaum, Michael. *The Dawn of Peace in Europe*. New York: Twentieth Century Fund, 1996.

McPherson, James M. *Battle Cry of Freedom*. New York: Oxford University Press, 1988.

Morton, H. V. *Atlantic Meeting*. New York: Dodd, Mead, 1943.

Murrow, Edward R. *In Search of Light*. New York: Knopf, 1967.

Neff, Donald. *Warriors at Suez*. New York: Linden Press/Simon and Schuster, 1981.

Newhouse, John. *De Gaulle and the Anglo-Saxons*. New York: Viking, 1970.

Nicholas, H. G. *The United States and Britain*. Chicago: University of Chicago Press, 1975.

Noble, Alexander. *From Rome to Maastricht*. London: Warner, 1996.

O'Clery, Conor. *The Greening of the White House*. Dublin: Gill and Macmillan, 1996.

Paul, Kathleen. *Whitewashing Britain*. Ithaca, NY: Cornell University Press, 1997.

Pells, Richard. *Not like Us*. New York: Basic Books, 1997.

Perkins, Bradford. *The Great Rapprochement*. New York: Atheneum, 1968.

———. *Prologue to War*. Berkeley: University of California Press, 1961.

Rentoul, John. *Tony Blair*. London: Little, Brown, 1995.

Renwick, Robin. *Fighting with Allies*. New York: Times Books, 1996.

Richelson, Jeffrey T., and Desmond Ball. *The Ties That Bind*. Boston: Allen and Unwin, 1985.

Rielly, John E. (ed.). *American Public Opinion and U.S. Foreign Policy, 1995*. Chicago: Chicago Council on Foreign Relations, 1995.

Shultz, George P. *Turmoil and Triumph*. New York: Scribner's, 1993.

Smith, Geoffrey. *Reagan and Thatcher*. New York: Norton, 1991.

Smith, James Morton (ed.). *The Republic of Letters*. New York: Norton, 1995.

Snowman, Daniel. *Britain and America: An Interpretation of Their Culture, 1945–1975*. New York: New York University Press, 1977.

Sosin, Jack M. *Agents and Merchants*. Lincoln: University of Nebraska Press, 1965.

Spender, Stephen. *Love-Hate Relations*. New York: Random House, 1974.

Stagg, J. C. A. *Mr. Madison's War*. Princeton: Princeton University Press, 1983.

Stares, Paul B. (ed.). *The New Germany and the New Europe*. Washington, DC: Brookings Institution, 1992.

Texas Department of Commerce, Business Development Division. *Foreign Direct Investment in Texas: Overview and Analysis*. Austin: Texas Department of Commerce, 1994.

Thatcher, Margaret. *The Downing Street Years*. New York: HarperCollins, 1993.

———. *The Path to Power*. New York: HarperCollins, 1995.

Thomas, Peter D. G. *Tea Party to Independence*. Oxford: Oxford University Press, 1991.

Toth, Robert C. *America's Place in the World, II*. Washington, DC: Pew Research Center for the People and the Press, 1997.

Trollope, Anthony. *Autobiography*. Oxford: Oxford University Press, 1992.

Trollope, Frances. *Domestic Manners of the Americans*. London: Folio Society, 1974.

Turner, Arthur Campbell. *The Unique Partnership: Britain and the United States*. New York: Bobbs-Merrill/Pegasus, 1971.

Ullman, Richard H. *Securing Europe*. Princeton: Princeton University Press, 1991.

Walker, Martin. *The President We Deserve*. New York: Crown, 1996.

Watt, D. Cameron. *Succeeding John Bull*. Cambridge: Cambridge University Press, 1984.

White, Theodore H. *Fire in the Ashes*. New York: Apollo Editions, 1968.

Wisniewski, Daniel (ed.). *Annual Abstract of Statistics: 1997 Edition*. London: Stationery Office, 1997.

Wistrich, Ernest. *The United States of Europe*. London: Routledge, 1994.

Woolcock, Stephen. *Market Access Issues in EC-US Relations*. London: Pinter/Royal Institute of International Affairs, 1991.

ARTICLES, PAPERS, DOCUMENTS, AND SPEECHES

Albright, Madeleine K. "Harvard University Commencement Address." *New York Times*, June 6, 1997, A8.

"The American Connection." *The Economist*, November 8, 1997, 63.

"Attitudes to the Falkland Islands." *British Public Opinion*, September 1995, 6.

Balladur, Edouard. "At the Crossroads." *The Economist*, March 1, 1997, 54–56.

Bergsten, C. Fred. "The Dollar and the Euro." *Foreign Affairs* 76, no. 4, July/August 1997, 83–95.

Blair, Tony. "Amsterdam Summit." Statement to the House of Commons, June 18, 1997.

———. "Northern Ireland." Speech to the Royal Ulster Agricultural Show, May 16, 1997.

Boshoff, Alison. "Baywatch Cues More Babes." *Daily Telegraph*, April 15, 1997, 12.

"Britain the Preferred Location." Invest in Britain Bureau, Department of Trade and Industry, November 1995.

"Britain's Overseas Trade." Foreign and Commonwealth Office, March 1994.

British Tourist Authority. "National Facts of Tourism." October 1996.

Brown, Gordon. "European and Economic Union." Statement to the House of Commons, October 27, 1997.

Clarity, James F. "Clinton's Role for Northern Ireland Talks: Restoring the Focus on the Big Picture." *New York Times*, December 5, 1995, A6.

———. "Protestants in Ulster Rebuke U.S." *New York Times*, September 11, 1997, A6.

Clarke, Kenneth. "Britain and the U.S." Speech to the Pilgrims Dinner, London, February 15, 1995.

Clinton, Bill. Speech to the citizens of Londonderry, Northern Ireland, November 30, 1995.

———. Speech to the Houses of Parliament, London, November 29, 1995.

———. Speech to the Irish Parliament, Dublin, December 1, 1995.

"Commercial Service—London: An Overview." United States Embassy, London, March 1997.

Cook, Robin. "British Foreign Policy: Mission Statement." Press conference, London, May 12, 1997.

———. "European Commission 'Agenda 2000' Communication." Statement issued July 16, 1997.

———. "European Security and Defense." Press conference at the WEU Ministerial Meeting, Paris, May 13, 1997.

Crowe, William J., Jr. "Transatlantic Relations and the Future of European Security." Speech to the Royal Institute of International Affairs, London, October 25, 1996.

Dornbusch, Rudi. "Monetary Union Might Just Put the Spring Back in Europe's Step." *Business Week*, December 23, 1996, 24.

Drozdiak, William. "How Not to Win Friends and Influence Europe." *Washington Post National Weekly Edition*, July 7, 1997, 18.

"Euro-apartheid?" *The Economist*, November 22, 1997, 55–56.

"Euro-philia." *The Economist*, July 19, 1997, 50.

"Focus on Britain." Foreign and Commonwealth Office, March 1996, 14.

"Free Trade and Foreign Policy: A Global Vision." Foreign and Commonwealth Office and Department of Trade and Industry, 1996.

"The Future of Europe." *British Public Opinion*, December 1996, 5.

"The Future of Warfare." *The Economist*, March 8, 1997, 15.

Garten, Jeffrey E. "America, Europe, and Germany: Commercial Relations for a New Era." Speech to the American Institute for Contemporary German Studies, New York, October 17, 1994.

Gates, Henry Louis, Jr. "Black London." *New Yorker*, April 28, 1997, 194–201.

"Germany's Eastward Urge." *The Economist*, March 15, 1997, 49.

"Global Defence Industry Survey." *The Economist*, June 14, 1997.

"Global Responses to Global Challenges." Press conference of Prime Minister Tony Blair and President Bill Clinton, London, May 29, 1997.

Gopnik, Adam. "The Culture of Blairism." *The New Yorker*, July 7, 1997, 26–32.

Grose, Thomas K. "Britain Rocks (Not Stonehenge)." *U.S. News and World Report*, March 3, 1997, 13.

Grunwald, Henry. "Jane Austen's Civil Society." *Wall Street Journal*, October 2, 1996, 20.

Henderson, Doug. "Britain and the E.U.—A Fresh Start." Speech to the EU Intergovernmental Conference Working Group of Personal Representatives, Brussels, May 5, 1997.

Hoge, Warren. "As British Rule in Hong Kong Fades, Rancor Sours Grandeur." *New York Times*, March 27, 1997, A1.

———. "Tory Leader Asks Delegates to Back a Conservatism That Cares." *New York Times*, October 11, 1997, A2.

Hurd, Douglas. "The Transatlantic Partnership." Speech to the Economic Club, the Chicago Council on Foreign Relations, and the Union League Club, Chicago, May 18, 1995.

Hutchings, Graham. "Britain Cast as the Villain in History of Hong Kong." *Daily Telegraph*, April 7, 1997, 12.

"Invest in Britain Bureau Review of Operations, 1996." Department of Trade and Industry, 1996.

Judt, Tony. "Continental Rift." *New York Times*, June 5, 1997, A21.

Katz, Ian. "Is Europe Elbowing the U.S. out of South America?" *Business Week*, August 4, 1997, 56.

Kerr, John. Untitled speech about U.S.-British relations, San Diego, California, December 13, 1996.

Kohut, Andrew, and Robert C. Toth. "Public Opinion and Trade Policy." News release, Times Mirror Center for the People and the Press, December 15, 1995.

————. "Trade and the Public." News release, Times Mirror Center for the People and the Press, December 13, 1994.

Lang, Ian. "Europe and America—Natural Partners." Speech to the European Institute, Washington, DC, November 8, 1995.

Lockwood, Christopher. "China Exposes the EU's Lack of Diplomacy." *Daily Telegraph*, April 21, 1997, 12.

Lohr, Steve. "Microsoft Picks England as Site of Research Lab." *New York Times*, June 18, 1997, C1.

Major, John. Speech about European security to WEU Parliamentary Assembly, London, February 23, 1996. Cited in *Survey of Current Affairs*, March 1996, 87.

Marchildon, Gregory P. "From Pax Britannica to Pax Americana and Beyond." *Annals of the American Academy of Political and Social Science* 538, March 1995, 151–168.

Martin, Laurence. "Risky Rush for a Doubtful Goal." *The World Today*, February 1997, 51–53.

"New Focus for the British Movie Industry." *Briefing on Britain* 1, no. 9, 1996, 12.

"New Labour's Model Army." *The Economist*, September 27, 1997, 61.

Nicolson, Nigel. "Jane Austen's Houses in Fact and Fiction." *Persuasions*, no. 14, 1992, 89.

"One Hundred Facts on London." London First Centre, June 1996.

"Public Indifferent about NATO Expansion." News release, Pew Research Center for the People and the Press, January 24, 1997.

Pushkov, Aleksei K. "The Risk of Losing Russia." *New York Times*, January 21, 1997, A19.

"Ready or Not, Here Comes EMU." *The Economist*, October 11, 1997, 21–23.

Reed, Stanley. "A Jolly Good Deal for Merrill Lynch." *Business Week*, December 1, 1997, 154.

Renwick, Robin. Speech to the Pilgrims Society, London, November 9, 1995.

Rifkind, Malcolm. "Europe: Which Way Forward?" Speech to the Konrad Adenauer Stiftung, Bonn, February 19, 1997.

————. "Principles and Practices of British Foreign Policy." Speech at Chatham House, London, September 21, 1995.

————. "Transatlantic Free Trade." Speech to the British-American Business Council, London, March 12, 1996.

————. "The Transatlantic Partnership: The Future Economic Agenda." Speech to the Transatlantic Policy Network, London, February 6, 1996.

Roberts, Roach, & Associates. "Economic Benefits of U.S.-U.K. Open Skies." Study prepared for American Airlines, Inc., October 1996.

Rohter, Larry. "Trade Storm Imperils Caribbean Banana Crops." *New York Times*, May 9, 1997, A6.

Ruhe, Volker. "New NATO, New Bundeswehr, and Peace in Bosnia and Herzegovina." *NATO Review*, May-June 1997, 4–7.

Sanger, David E. "Hong Kong's Business Elite Tells Americans: Don't Panic." *New York Times*, June 5, 1997, A1.

Santer, Jacques. "Britain's Rightful Place." *The Economist*, May 10, 1997, 50–51.

Sapsted, David. "Britain Guilty of Genocide, Says Governor." *Daily Telegraph*, October 17, 1996, 20.

Schmidt, Gustav. "Historical Traditions and the Inevitability of European Ties." *Annals of the American Academy of Political and Social Science* 538, March 1995, 83–95.

Schmidt, Helmut. "Miles to Go." *Foreign Affairs* 76, no. 3, May/June 1997, 213–221.

Seitz, Raymond. Speech to the Pilgrims Society, London, April 19, 1994.

Simms, Calvin. "Free-Trade Zone of the Americas Given the Go-Ahead." *New York Times*, April 20, 1998, A1.

Smith, Roland. "A Changing NATO." *NATO Review*, May-June 1997, 8–11.

Steel, Ronald. "Mission Creep." *New Republic*, November 25, 1996, 29.

Stevenson, Jonathan. "Northern Ireland: Treating Terrorists as Statesmen." *Foreign Policy*, no. 105, Winter 1996–97, 125–140.

Szulc, Tad. "A Looming Greek Tragedy in Hong Kong." *Foreign Policy*, no. 106, Spring 1997, 77–89.

Thatcher, Margaret. "Reason and Religion: The Moral Foundations of Freedom." James Bryce Lecture on the American Commonwealth, Institute of United States Studies, University of London, 1996.

Tugend, Alina. "A British Boom in American Studies." *Chronicle of Higher Education*, April 14, 1995, A40–41.

"UK Will Take All Appropriate Steps to Protect Its Trading Interests (Helms-Burton Legislation)." British Information Services press release, May 3, 1996.

Wallace, William. "On the Move—Destination Unknown." *The World Today*, April 1997, 99–102.

Whitney, Craig R. "Civil Strife Has NATO Facing Demons Within." *New York Times*, July 6, 1997, 4.

Worcester, Robert M. "Attitudes to America, Americans, American Foreign and Defense Policy, and to American Multinational Companies in Britain." Paper presented to conference on "The American Presence in Britain," Institute of United States Studies, Regent's College, London, 1989.

Wrobel, Paulo. "Towards a Beautiful Horizon?" *The World Today*, May 1997, 134–135.

INDEX

About the Author

PHILIP SEIB is Professor of Journalism at Southern Methodist University and a veteran television and newspaper journalist. He is the author of nine books, most recently, *Headline Diplomacy: How News Coverage Affects Foreign Policy* (Praeger, 1997).